The Present in Delhi's Pasts

The Present in Delhi's Pasts

Five Essays

Second Edition, Revised and Updated

Sunil Kumar

Three Essays
COLLECTIVE

Third printing November 2022
Second Revised Edition January 2011
First published under the imprint Three Essays Press in 2002

ISBN 978-81-88789-44-3

Three Essays
COLLECTIVE

B-957 Palam Vihar, GURGAON (Haryana) 122 017 India
Phone: 91-124 2369023, +91 98681 26587, +91 98683 44843
info@threeessays.com Website: www.threeessays.com
Printed and bound at Chaman Offset Printers, New Delhi

For M-36 and a home full of memories.

Contents

Contents

Preface to the Second Edition

Travellers to South Delhi might see two interesting monuments – one new and the other old. The new one is in Saket, in the middle of a newly laid out park by the edge of the fortifications of the first Sultanate city. It is a statue of Prithviraj Chauhan, and the old ruined city is rather casually referred to by scholars and laypersons alike, as Qila Ra'i Pithora, the fort of Prithviraj Chauhan. The park and statue were laid out during the Lieutenant-Governorship of Jagmohan Mishra, a senior member of the Bharatiya Janata Party. He wanted to create a resplendent capital, with wide boulevards, green parks, well identified heritage spots and a clean environment. Nothing particularly wrong with any of these goals except that in Jagmohan's vision the inhabitants of the city needed to be cleansed and sanitised until all those responsible for the mess that the city was in – the underprivileged, the low castes and the non-Hindu – were marginalised on its outskirts.

In the construction of the park and statue it did not cross Jagmohan's mind that the medieval city that he had appropriated as Qila Ra'i Pithora had nothing to do with Prithviraj's capital at all. Prithviraj's capital was Ajmer not Delhi. This was the capital of Delhi Sultans like Iltutmish, Balban and 'Ala' al-Din Khalaji and known as Dihli-i kuhna, or "Old Delhi". Govind Ra'i, the governor of Prithviraj (not Prithviraj himself), had his small fort near Mehrauli called Lal Kot. Interesting details, but do they matter?

To gauge the full significance of these stories, travel to the second and much older monument in South Delhi, the Qutb Minar. If you are a tourist and know nothing about the place there is a good likelihood that you will hire a tour guide, accredited by the Archaeological Survey of India, no less. The gentlemen (they are generally, all men) carry with them a patronizing air of authority; these are venerable historians who will, for a paltry sum of money, educate you about the mysteries of the strange monuments before you. Over the next hour and a half you will hear about Prithviraj's temple, his Vijaysthamb (his victory tower -- the Qutb minar), built for Prithviraj's daughter so that she could perform her sun worship while facing the Jumna every morning. The details of Muslim iconoclasm would be laid bare even as the details of the old Hindu temple (not Jain, mind you) are carefully drawn out. By the time the visitor leaves the Qutb precincts, the area would appear as the cradle of Hindu civilization vandalized by foreign Muslim invaders. That the Government of India should honour its glorious past by raising a statue to Prithviraj Chauhan would appear, then, as a fairly normal, nationalist thing to do.

It would be a mistake to assume that the writing of these local histories comes from simple ignorance – non-professional historians recapturing the past without much attention to "facts" or sensitivity to the production of evidence. The writing of history is not the monopoly of professional historians alone. As the events relating to the demolition of the Babri Masjid or the American invasion of Iraq have clarified, the common-place renditions of the past need to be taken very seriously because the world acts on the basis of these interpretations and not the academic tomes or the debates that grip our universities. To understand how the subject of Prithviraj Chauhan has a larger resonance, for example, notice how the Government of India decided to name its Inter Regional Ballistic

Missile (IRBM) "Prithvi" after the famous Rajput ruler who had defended Delhi from "foreign" Muslim invasions. That these are not matters of arcane historical details but great geopolitics was evident in Pakistan's riposte: they named their IRBM "Ghauri" after Mu'izz al-Din Ghuri, whose generals had captured and ruled from Delhi. Had the fate of billions of people not been involved this could have passed as name calling in a school yard fracas!

Historians as they write about the past have their feet firmly planted in the present. It is the debates of their immediate world that often provide them with questions and issues, the language and the metaphors which they use in their research. The essays in this volume are strongly touched by the politics of the 1980s and 1990s: the anti-Sikh riots in Delhi, the Mandal commission, the Hindutva mobilisation, the disjunctions cause by economic reform, the push to modernity and India's search for a global influence. These subjects may seem incredibly remote from the concerns that should grip a medieval historian, but they were not. So much of the communal rhetoric and hatred that grips India today resides upon well integrated assumptions about monolithic community identities and the impact of the omnipresent state on the lives of Indians. In medieval studies, not only are Hindus and Muslims cast within homogenous categories but the state is equally monochromatic: a Hindu or a Muslim state, and, as alternatives, a centralised in contrast to an effete decentralised one. As I queried the historiographies on which these readings were grounded, I discovered I was also challenging so much of the rhetoric on which the politics of the present was mobilised. This book is about the present in Delhi's pasts but it is equally about the pasts in the city's present. And since we are still uncertain about where "history will take us next" – a different take on how history, and the past and present are connected – these essays were penned with a great concern about the future.

I am grateful to the Three Essays Collective for bringing out a second edition of these essays and for the indulgence they showed in including an additional essay.

Sunil Kumar

Saket, New Delhi, July 2010

Introduction

To think of Delhi today is to imagine a city with a geographical span almost the size of greater Chicago and a population nearly equal to New York, a city that was a capital, much like London, of a dominant political formation in north India for nearly a millenium. In much of the literature of the past and the present, Delhi seems to be almost coterminous with India; the making of the state and the city often appears inextricably intertwined. It takes considerable skill to actually disaggregate this history, to imagine a Delhi (leave alone a state) that was not always of this size.

In 1947 and independence, the modern capital of New Delhi occupied an extremely small area. For the better part, the plain of South Delhi was an agricultural tract. Walled medieval cities, the capitals of the Sultans of Delhi, large and small, only occupied a portion of the 'plain of Delhi'. There were also a plethora of villages in this tract of land, some with a history of residence much older than the medieval towns.

We are better informed today – if still rather simplistically – about the history of the walled cities of the rulers of Delhi. The rise and decline of dynasties paralleled the fate of their capitals. Lofty citadels ignored by succeeding dynasties crumbled into disrepair and became the haunt of pastoralists, palaces were reapportioned into dwellings of peasants, villages sprouted on old parade grounds and along city gates. Epitaphs of the medieval cities of Delhi seldom wandered from this script. Ozymandias-like, the ruins stood as testimony to the fate of proud rulers whose accomplishments lay in ruins.

Three essays in this volume (Chapters I-III) relate to areas in New Delhi that date from the twelfth through the fourteenth centuries, the period of the Delhi Sultans. They are about sites in South Delhi that I first visited in the 1970's as I developed my interests in medieval history during graduate study My wife and I would cycle to these sites and spend hours wandering through the ruins. In the 1980's, as a teacher at St. Stephens and later the history department at Delhi University, I revisited these areas. I was now a father, leading adventurous expeditions into the unknown, having a great time with my daughter and son. I was mixing pleasure with business. Many of the sites that I visited were in relatively obscure villages. I wondered if it was possible to interweave their histories in my classes, bring my subject more alive to a body of students falling fast asleep with a surfeit of lectures on Sultanate campaigns and Mughal revenue administrative systems.

My interest in these areas continued through the decade and overlapped with my research on the Delhi Sultans. It was exhilarating to discover stray episodes relating to the early history of these sites even as I worked on a more recondite history of the Sultanate. My long interaction with these sites also gave me a chance to notice changes that they were undergoing and to reflect upon the interface between the past and the present. As it turned out, I was no longer just a medieval historian visiting old ruins but also a chronicler, noticing and recording developments that were apparent in these villages.

The 1980's, especially after the 1982 Asian Games, introduced a period of extraordinary change in New Delhi. These were, on the one hand, salutary signs of 'progress' brought about by efforts to modernise, develop municipal services and an appearance befitting the nation's capital. There was a complacent pride in the air even as the nation and its middle class seemed to be coming into its own at the end of the millenium. The tragic events of 1984 and 1992, however, underlined the presence of other, more xenophobic nationalistic currents that were also very much a parcel of the city's and the nation's drive towards modernity.

In the last decades of the twentieth century, years after independence, the nation seems to have renewed a search for its identity and its roots. History textbooks are subjects of debate and revision, Hindutva ideologues and globalism increasingly threaten the country's pluralistic cultures. The pasts of the subcontinent are a threat to the manner in which some would want to shape its present. As I wandered through the medieval villages of New Delhi I was struck by the sheer longevity of documented human interaction that some of these sites had witnessed. Many of these places had seen continuous human habitation for a millenium. They had complex histories of demographic changes, shifting political associations and ideological formations. While these areas had experienced their share of violent transitions, their pasts were equally layered with years of peace. It was a rich heritage, but an embarrassing, dangerous one for a modern audience looking for simple, linear correlations between the past and the present to legitimate narrow, presentist interests.

The essays in this volume are about old monuments and villages in New Delhi, some of which few have ever heard about. Others are extremely well known. But underlying all these essays is the larger conundrum of how we need to face our pasts without erasing them. I hope the essays in this book will serve to communicate the urgency of this issue.

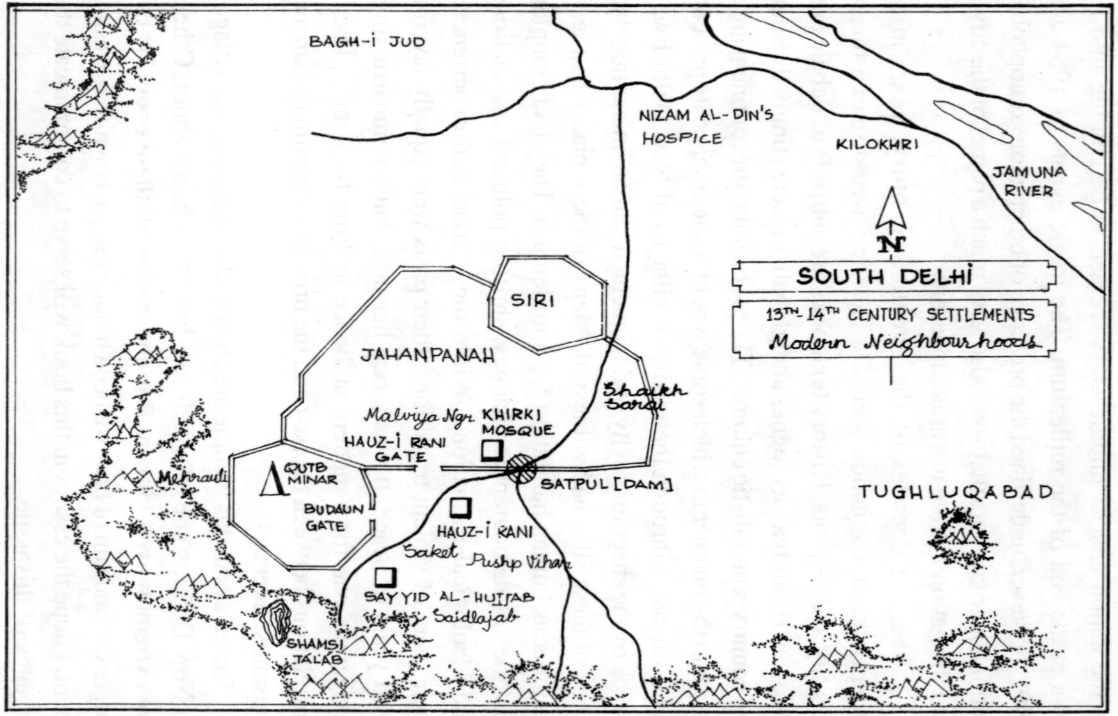

SOUTH DELHI
13TH-14TH CENTURY SETTLEMENTS
Modern Neighbourhoods
N
BAGH-I JUD
NIZAM AL-DIN'S HOSPICE
KILOKHRI
JAMUNA RIVER
SIRI
JAHANPANAH
Shaikh Sarai
Malviya Ngr.
KHIRKI MOSQUE
HAUZ-I RANI GATE
QUTB MINAR
Mehrauli
SATPUL [DAM]
TUGHLUQABAD
BUDAUN GATE
HAUZ-I RANI
Saket
Pushp Vihar
SAYYID AL-HUJJAB
Saidlajab
SHAMSI TALAB

Quṭb and Modern Memory[1]

The Quṭb *mīnār* and mosque, Delhi's first *masjid-i jāmi'* constructed in the last decade of the twelfth century, has drawn the attention of tourists, antiquarians and scholars over the years. The tall minaret with its elaborate balconies and intricate inscriptions has an element of what Gell called "magic".[2] How did people in the late twelfth and early thirteenth centuries construct something so enormous, so perfectly symmetrical, and yet so delicate? Our cultural sensibilities attuned to appreciate uniqueness, size, proportion and the investment of money and labour, savour the immensity and beauty of the structure and marvel at the accomplishment of mortals nearly a millenium ago. The reactions of visitors to the adjoining mosque, constructed out of the rubble of twenty-seven demolished temples, are, however, more ambivalent. The starkness of the mosque is relieved only by the redeployed temple spoils. Temple columns, Hindu and Jain iconic motifs, some complete and many defaced idols, are beautiful in themselves but clearly out of context within the environs of the mosque. They appear to be spoils of war, the evidence of pillage and victory in a conflict fought in the distant past. Most visitors to the mosque today are unaware of the identity of the contestants nor are the events of the conflict any clearer. But since the presence of plundered material from "Hindu" temples within a "Muslim" mosque is unmistakeable, the masjid confirms images of Islamic iconoclasm, and fanaticism. It resurrects memories of communal distinctions and strife which almost every Indian regards as a part of his and her country's social history. Unlike the minaret, the mosque impresses visitors with its images of destruction, power and might, but not "magic".

The manner in which visitors to the Quṭb complex understand and interpret the structures at the site is not simply shaped by their cognitive understanding of what constitutes an object of "beauty". It is as much a product of their socialised, historicised, understanding of the intentions of the constructors, and the meanings they presume are encoded into the structure. This paper seeks to study the manner in which the Quṭb complex is understood today, and the epistemological assumptions which have supported such a conclusion. As I discuss in my paper, a host of significations were attached to the mosque by its builders and detractors in the Middle Ages and many of these were reworked in the popular imagination in the early modern period. Yet, today, one interpretation has survived through the ages and dominated all others.

Historians have played a major rôle in the construction of this modern memory of the Quṭb. They have written extensively on the Quṭb itself, and on the political and religious conditions of the time when it was built. Their research on the Quṭb, however, has not remained relegated to the pages of arcane tomes; it has received wide circulation in text books and the popular press. Daily, thousands of visitors are guided through the Quṭb monuments by the descriptions and interpretations provided by the Archaeological Survey of India at the site of the mosque itself. These narratives were culled from the works of scholars on medieval architecture, Islam and Indian history. Together they constitute a text through which the experience of visitors to one of the major tourist spots in north India is refracted into authoritative knowledge about the character of Islamic piety and the nature of "Muslim rule" in medieval India.

This paper enlarges on the complex relationship between scholastic interpretations and popular perceptions in the constitution of the Quṭb complex as a statement of the "Might of Islam" in India. An interpretation which unfortunately consolidates the fractured communal realities of a post- partition subcontinent.

I. The Delhi *masjid-i jāmi'*, its builders, and its main features[3]

The Delhi *masjid-i jāmi'* underwent construction on three different occasions. The first mosque, 214 by 149 feet, was a relatively small rectangular structure, with a central courtyard surrounded by colonnaded arcades. The construction of the mosque was commenced in 587/1191-2 by Quṭb al-Dīn Ai-Beg, and relied upon material derived from plundered temples. The temple spoils were used randomly, but very ingeniously, within the mosque. Column shafts, bases, and capitals, of different sizes and forms, with Hindu or Jain sculptures and iconic motifs, were placed one upon the other to attain a uniform height for the roof. The lack of concern for iconic symmetry, with Shaivite, Vaishnavite and Jain motifs placed cheek-by-jowl with each other, conveys the impression of destruction, a temper which is very much a part of the construction of the first mosque. The Archaeological Survey of India helps in the consolidation of this impression. Through its tourist literature it reminds visitors that the better portion of the mosque resides on the plinth of a demolished temple. Together with other evidence of redeployment of plundered material, the visitor is left to assume that the "iron pillar" of the Gupta period was another trophy of conquest placed within the centre of the mosque by Muslim invaders.[4]

Sometime later, perhaps in 595/1199, the huge arched screen was built in front of the west wall of the mosque. The east face of the screen was decorated with Arabic calligraphy, verses from the *Qur'ān* and the traditions of the Prophet, interspersed with floral and geometric patterns. Perhaps even more dramatically than the reused temple spoils, the screen carries evidence of the handiwork of native artisans, who used familiar traditions of corbelled architecture to satisfy unusual stylistic requirements. It was around this time that work on the ground floor of the minaret was also completed. Although derived from the architectural precedents established in the Ghūrid minaret of Khwājā Siyah Pūsh in Sistan, the *mīnār*, in Quṭb al-Dīn's reign, was not very tall, and its girth lent it a rather squat appearance. Built out of red sandstone and inscribed with *Qur'ānic* inscriptions and eulogies of conquest it served as a memorial of victory and a vantage point to call the faithful to prayer.

The second phase of construction within the *masjid-i jāmi'* occured during the reign of Shams al-Dīn Iltutmish (607-33/1210-36) and was completed sometime around 627/1229-30. Although Iltutmish's additions nearly doubled the width, if not the depth, of the mosque, very little survives today of this construction. New courtyards were added to the north, south and the east, in a form which maintained the overall stylistic symmetry of the mosque. Hence the arches and the additions to the minaret harmonised with the preexisting architecture. Since these additions are largely in ruins today, the final impact of their size and grandeur, their dwarfing of the original *masjid*, is completely lost upon the modern audience. Only the extended minaret, towering over the environs with three additional storeys, provides a sense of the huge transformation that Iltutmish introduced in the architectural landscape of the *masjid-i jāmi'*. Many historians tend to obscure this intervention by suggesting that rather than altering the mosque, Iltutmish merely "completed" it.[5]

The changes in the mosque introduced during the third phase of construction, in the reign of 'Alā' al-Dīn Khalajī (695-715/1296-1316), are also nearly lost today. But for one entrance hall, and an unfinished minaret, there is no visible trace of any Khalajī building activity within the mosque. Archaeological evidence, however, has clarified that 'Alā' al-Dīn extended the mosque until it was twice the size of Iltutmish's, that the arches on its west wall towered over the older constructions, and if the girth of the unfinished *mīnār* is any indication, it would also have been twice the size of the old. Other than the size, the entrance hall on the south wall, today called the "ʿAlā'ī darwaza", stands as a testimony to the quality of construction during this period. Built out of red sandstone, the square silhouette of the "darwaza" is pierced with evenly spaced rectangular windows and doors. These are outlined with marble trimmings and epigraphs carrying *Qur'ānic* verses and statements commemorating the achievements of the Sultan. The modern visitor needs to imagine, if he or she can, a rite of passage from the bustling world of the medieval city of Delhi, through the ornate "ʿAlā'ī darwaza" into the relative peace of the enormous Khalajī mosque, with huge arches decorated with *Qur'ānic* verses on the western wall, a new minaret under construction to balance and dwarf the old one. In sheer size and grandeur it would have been one of the most prepossessing mosques of its time in the world.

Since the middle of the nineteenth century, scholars and archaeologists have studied this mosque and attempted to explain its significance to a lay audience. Their writings have over the years assumed "authoritative dimensions", until most visitors rely upon their guidance to consolidate their own opinions of the structure. The next section attempts to disaggregate this scholarship to understand how changing historical assumptions and research methodologies are reflected in the study of the Quṭb monuments.

II. Reading the *masjid-i jāmiʿ* as the Might of Islam mosque

The *munṣif* of Delhi, Sayyid Ahmad Khan, was the first scholar to make a detailed study of the epigraphs and architectural form of the Quṭb complex in the 1840's. Many of his conclusions were summarised and developed in the reports of the Archaeological Survey of India written in the 1860's, and some years later in the *Epigraphica Indo-Moslemica*, a journal devoted to the study of Persian and Arabic inscriptions. Much of this information was recompiled in the 1920's in the report of the excavations and conservation efforts of the Archaeological Survey of India narrated by J.A. Page. This corpus of information provided the empirical data on the basis of which an early consensual opinion on the nature of the Quṭb complex developed.[6] The guides prepared at the turn of the century for English tourists to Delhi also relied upon these scholarly texts for their information and interpretation.

The major subject of interest in the works of all these authors was the redeployment of Hindu and Jain temple material within the *masjid* structure. Their narrative and line drawings focused upon the details of this aspect of the congregational mosque: what was the extent of the original plinth of the temple upon which the mosque was built; how many temple pillars were in fact used in the making of the cloisters? Alternatively their attention was drawn to the fact that "Hindu" architectural styles continued to predominate within a "Muslim" mosque. They noted the absence of the true arch in the great screen of the mosque and the usage of a corbelled technique together with the *voussoir* by indigenous craftsmen to convey the impression of the "saracenic" arch. In a similar fashion these scholars also noted the inability of the "Hindu" craftsmen to construct domes; instead "domes" which once again followed the corbelled technique were used from despoiled temples. Their discussion of the minaret was again largely restricted to its stylistic origins: was it of a "Hindu" provenance, or did it have earlier G͟hūrid and G͟haznavid antecedents?

Khan, Cunningham and Page's analysis suggested that in the usage of plundered temple material, which was defaced, inverted, or plastered over, the military commander, Quṭb al-Dīn Ai-Beg, made a statement of conquest and hegemony over an infidel population in north India, and conducted a ritual cleansing of profane territory. The authors also recognised the presence of temple material in the mosque as an evidence of a swift transposition of "Muslim rule" in "India" where the "Turkish cavalry" had outdistanced the "Muslim artisans".

Architecture in the formal "Saracenic" tradition, constructed under the supervision of immigrant "Muslim architects" and craftsmen had to, therefore, await the later years of Iltutmi<u>sh</u>'s reign (607-33/1210-36). Meanwhile the symbolic redeployment of plundered temple rubble in the *masjid-i jāmi'*, did not merely proclaim Quṭb al-Dīn's conquest of Delhi (588/1192), it also served as a statement of Islam's victory over idolators. This point was driven home when Sayyid Ahmad Khan, Horowitz and Page recorded in their respective scholarly publications that the name by which the congregational mosque was known in the past was *"Quwwat al-Islām"*, or the "Might of Islam". Their self confident assertion was surprising for the *masjid-i jāmi'* was not identified as *Quwwat al-Islām* by any extant inscription in the mosque or referred by this name in any Sultanate chronicle.[7] As we will see later it was a corruption of a name sometimes used for Delhi in the thirteenth century. Suffice it to note for now, that for these scholars, it was almost logical that the congregational mosque which celebrated the conquest of Delhi should be called the "Might of Islam". After all, the conquest of Delhi, the capital of the Sultanate, was the final, victorious culmination of a preceding series of plunder raids led by "Muslims" into Sind, Punjab, and "Hindustan". In the early narrative of Indian history, where the medieval period was synonymous with the Muslim, it was entirely apposite that Delhi's first *masjid-i jāmi'* should be named the *Quwwat al-Islām* mosque, and symbolise the beginning of a new historical epoch.

In the 1960's when a more "secular" narration of the South Asian medieval past was attempted, historians like Meister, Mujeeb and later Husain glossed over the "Might of Islam" interpretation of the masjid.[8] Their writings focused instead upon the architectural characteristics of the monument where Islamic inspiration was dependent upon indigenous craftsmanship for its ultimate realisation. In an effort to mute the episode of plunder and military conquest involved in the capture of Delhi, the "Hindu" adaptation of the "saracenic arch", or the corbelled dome, were highlighted as examples of inter-community cooperation and amity. Although these scholars continued to accept the interpretation of the *masjid* as the *Quwwat al-Islām*, their writings suggested that this might have been merely a formal statement not to be taken very seriously. To their mind, the presence of the Hindu hand in designing and constructing the mosque should be given greater recognition.

Anthony Welch and Robert Hillenbrand could not disagree more with such "secular" interpretations of the mosque.[9] Writing in the 1990's, these scholars are strongly influenced by the cultural anthropological emphasis upon semiotics and ideology. Unlike scholars in the past, who were presumably guided by their anachronistic communal or secular assumptions, these scholars sought the "native's point of view", a potentially more dangerous interpretive move in its assumption that it could capture an indigenous, native perspective. Welch found it significant that the Muslim patrons of the Hindu craftsmen never compromised with the indigenes: the Delhi Sultans forced the Hindu craftsmen in their service to always conform to a "Muslim aesthetic". In an important passage he noted that "the architecture of this early Turkish-dominated period is not eclectic: instead it is obsessed with imposing an aesthetic that carried comforting meaning for the conquerors. The attempt to replicate the familiar from back home is overriding: it ignores north India's established building types and twists indigenous architectural techniques to accomodate it. The resulting torque is obvious, but not surprising: without such mimetic references the [Delhi] Sultanate would have appeared adrift in an all too new and unfamiliar land".[10]

In his study of the epigraphical remains in the congregational mosque, the *mīnār*, and Iltutmi<u>sh</u>'s tomb, Welch concluded that the inscriptions were carefully located within the *masjid-i jāmi'* precincts bearing in mind the architectural and functional qualities of the specific structures. Thus, since the *mīnār* performed the "symbolic function of marking the *Dār al-Islām* (the land of Islam)" newly conquered from the infidels, and the towering structure was "most visible to believers and non-believers outside the city walls", it carried *Qur'ānic* statements of conquest and warning to the heathen population.[11] The *Qur'ānic* and *ḥadīs̱* inscriptions on the *qiblah* screen, the direction all Muslims faced during prayer, stressed "instead the importance of worship, of adherence to the principles of Islam, and of recognition of the obligations incumbent on believers". While the *mīnār* was directed primarily to the "Hindus" and its epigraphs proclaimed victory over heathens, the inscriptions within the sanctuary of the *masjid-i jāmi'* were addressed only to the Muslims and expounded "general religious statements" concerning their conduct.[12]

Welch's analysis of the congregational mosque and its epigraphs was not far removed from that of Khan, Cunningham or Page. While the latter had emphasised the theme of Muslim conquest and victory symbolised by the Quṭb monument, Welch developed the idea further and argued that the congregational mosque also reflected the political context in which it was created. The monument was an uncompromising Muslim celebration of conquest, and the building material, architectural forms and epigraphic texts of the congregational mosque asserted the unity and cultural uniqueness of the "Muslims". It distanced the conquerors from their "Hindu" subjects while creating familiar, reassuring landmarks of Islam's superiority for Muslims resident in a "foreign" land.[13] From a different methodological track, Welch confirmed that the Quṭb complex needed to be understood as the "Might of Islam".

III. Providing the political context

Welch could push his reading of "the native's point of view" with a great deal of confidence because his arguments coincided with, and were supported by, a larger historiographical interpretation of the nature of early Sultanate society and polity in north India. In the early thirteenth century, according to the author, the Turkic ruling class of the Sultanate was both "compact and cohesive", and severely threatened by "Hindu" opposition. The historiographical understanding of the bonds which tied the Delhi Sultan with his military commanders were worked out in the writings of a number of authors which included scholars of the stature of Habibullah, Nizami, and Nigam.[14] In the interpretations of these scholars, despite the occasions when the "crown and the nobility" were in conflict, an underlying material self interest, a shared Turkish ethnicity, and the religion of Islam, provided coherence and an exclusive nature to the Turkic ruling oligarchy in the thirteenth century. In this logic, the common background of the ruling elite and their Sultan made them a category apart, and in the absence of any shared affinities with the ruler, the "Hindus" were a distinct group who were then treated indifferently as subjects. The equation, Muslim rule = Muslim state, was worked out to its full extent in the writings of Habibullah, who completed the juxtaposition by defining resistance to the Sultanate as "Hindu aggression".[15] In Welch's analysis this was summed up in his declaration that "with their victory in 1192...[the Muslim armies]...initiated an Islamic state that by the beginning of the fourteenth century encompassed nearly all of the Indian subcontinent."[16]

In this vision of medieval history it was also argued that by the fourteenth century the composition of the Muslim ruling elite began to alter until it started to include "low class" indigenous Muslim converts, a process which one scholar described as the "plebianization of the nobility".[17] The presence of these neo-convert indigenes provided the Sultanate with cultural "roots" in the subcontinent.[18] This was most apparent in art, architecture, literature, and ritual; but it did not affect the great chasm which separated the politically cohesive, rapacious Muslim state from the exploited peasantry. The juxtaposition of the monolithic entities – the rulers and the ruled – was perceived by scholars as an axiomatic reality throughout the middle ages. With regard to the establishment of the Delhi Sultanate, Irfan Habib, perhaps the most influential scholar writing on medieval India, noted:

> The Ghorian conquests of Northern India, leading to the establishment of the Delhi Sultanate (1206-1526) may be said to mark the true beginning of the medieval period in India...To begin with, the new conquerors and rulers, who were of a different faith (Islam) from that of their predecessors, established a regime that was in some profound respects different from the old. The Sultans achieved power that was, in terms of both territorial extent and centralisation, unprecedented (except, perhaps, for the Mauryas 1,500 years earlier)...[Centralisation]... ensured that the land revenue (*kharāj/māl*) demanded on their behalf should comprehend the bulk, if not the whole, of the peasant's surplus produce; and the King's bureaucracy thereby became the principal exploiting class in society.[19]

Habib shifted the argument of his peers to suggest that the fundamental contradiction within the medieval political systems constructed by Muslims in south Asia derived from class and not confessional interests. Yet, despite the presence of a variety of class interests, it was the fundamental divide between the rulers and the ruled which determined the fate of the state. In Habib's argument, the binary relationship between the extractive state and oppressed peasantry was initiated by the Delhi Sultans, but finessed under the Mughal emperor Akbar (963-1014/1556-1605). "The peculiar feature of the State in Mughal India -- indeed, in Medieval India", according to Habib, "was that it served not merely as the protective arm of the exploiting classes, but was itself the principal instrument of exploitation."[20] Habib's description of the Mughal state as an instrument of class oppression also led him to define the Mughal *manṣabdārī* corp as the primary exploitative class.

Irfan Habib's reading of the Sultanate and Mughal political systems had a huge impact on the field of medieval studies. It was evident in the work of Tapan Raychaudhuri, the co-editor (along with Irfan Habib) of the *Cambridge Economic History of India*, who expanded these arguments: "For the indigenous population in many parts of the sub-continent, the Mughal empire was a machine to extract resources to be consumed or hoarded by a small number of aliens, with a share of the spoils going to the native ruling class".[21] Raychaudhuri had also pointed out that "...for the Hindu population in general the imperial services were not something they could aspire to. ...fresh recruitment to the ruling class was restricted mainly to alien social groups".[22] Not all historians put the matter so bluntly but it was not a huge distance to travel once there was a general agreement amongst scholars regarding the presence of a homogenous Mughal ruling class.

Originating from a completely different set of epistemes, the implications of this analysis was very close to Habibullah's (and Welch's) conclusions. Despite differing methodological perspectives, both Habibullah and Habib agreed that the cohesive unity of the state was never challenged by its participants. Habibullah argued for a hostile relationship between the Muslim Turkic ruling elite and the Hindu subject population, and for Habib, a variety of class contradictions notwithstanding, the significant divide remained the one between the exploiters and the exploited. Although the "hostile relationships" and "class contradictions" derived from different reasons, their implications for the state and the ruling elite were very similar. Just as Habibullah had suggested that "dynastic troubles and rebellions" might have temporarily weakened the state during the inter-regnal years of the early Sultanate, but "Hindu aggression" threatened and challenged its structure, Habib argued that the Mughal "Empire never really faced a serious revolt from within the ranks of its own bureaucracy...[and]... the major upheavals... caused by the wars of succession...did not by themselves endanger the Mughal throne."[23] Hence, when the tyranny of the exploitative state resulted in agrarian distress, peasant forces, sometimes led by *zamīndār*s, were ranged against the state mechanism. It was the politically "disenfranchised", the outsiders, that endangered the state. In the analysis of the two authors, at least this aspect of the medieval state system did not alter dramatically through the Sultanate into the Mughal period.

IV. Positivistic readings of the text

In a historiography where the material interests of the monolithic state were threatened only by the exploited, conquered indigenous population, the discursive assertions of the authority of the state were read as reaffirmations of the existing [class] solidarity of the ruling elite. What was lost in reading a text from this perspective was the recognition that discursive texts, like Delhi's thirteenth century *masjid-i jāmi'*, carried the authorial voice of their patrons, the Delhi Sultans, and they would have hardly acknowledged the presence of competing centres of power or resistance in a monument that was a public statement of their authority. In a similar fashion it was hardly likely that the court chroniclers of the Delhi Sultans would organise their narratives to suggest that Delhi was not the legitimate centre of power and authority in north India. In the Persian chronicles of Minhāj-i Sirāj Jūzjānī, Ẓiyā' al-Dīn Baranī or Abū' al-Faẓl, the power of the monarch might be challenged by his subordinates – as it certainly was when rulers were morally incompetent – but the occasional hiatus notwithstanding, there was never any alternative to the authority of Delhi or the Mughal *Pādshāh*.

Since the 1960s historians of the medieval period have shown increasing care in their usage of primary sources, and have stopped taking literally the encomiums paid to their masters by court chroniclers. Such a literalness was largely a result of positivistic emphases of the historian's craft, where greater attention was paid to ascertaining "facts" from "unimpeachable sources". In his "defence" of Baranī's *Ta'rīkh-i Fīrūz Shāhī*, Habib explained his argument: "first, that Baranī's factual account is correct in all substantive matters; and secondly, that, though the 'analysis' is his (Baranī's) own, it is nevertheless sound...".[24] In the same historiographical tradition, Shireen Moosvi worked out the reasons to believe in Abū' al-Faẓl's veracity: "Abu'l Faẓl in his conclusion to the *Ā'īn* tells us of the way he collected the material for his work. He says that his information was based on the testimony of contemporaries and eyewitnesses, after a critical assessment of whatever they had said...for the *Ā'īn-i Akbarī* he relied practically entirely upon state papers, and his statistical data were, naturally, supplied by government departments. He tells us he revised the text five times...".[25]

Most contemporary scholars forget, however, that the medieval documentation used by them, either chronicler or archival, was either produced by or for the state. For them, once we sift the encomia from these texts we remove the obvious elements of bias, and are left with a largely unaltered narrative in which the king and his subordinates remained the principal actors in the history of the period. In a sense, as in the case of Ranke himself, the search for "authoritative information" in chronicles and archives privileged the knowledge conveyed by the written word which, for the medieval period, concerned the state and governance. Information from other authors was understood to be biased unless it corroborated the product of the state. In his study of the Sikh sacred text, the *Guru Granth Sahib*, Habib argued that "my purpose has been to suggest that research for material of historical value in this popular religious literature of medieval times may not altogether be an unfruitful pursuit. But it should be borne in mind at the same time that such research should go hand in hand with a close study of the Persian evidence as well, for only a familiarity with the latter can help us to pick out information that is *really* of significance (my emphasis) in the source-material in local languages."[26] If research is going to privilege information produced by the state and then look for its corroboration from other sources, Athar Ali's conclusion is hardly surprising: "fresh explorations of documentary evidence have only tended to confirm and underline the standard proposition about the elements of centralisation and systemisation in the Mughal polity..." and "the picture of the Mughal Empire in its classic phase, as centralised polity, geared to systematisation and creation of an all imperial bureaucracy, ...still remain[s] unshaken".[27]

The positivist methodology which exalted documents as the pristine sources for the study of the past directed scholars of medieval India to seek in their Persian documentation the secrets of the middle ages. But a Rankean epistemology, which elevated the state as the epitome of historical development and the proper subject of historical investigation, also led them to accept the discourse of a unitary dominion, a cohesive ruling elite, and a potentially recalcitrant peasantry without any critical reflection. It is this epistemology which enables the reading of the Quṭb monuments today as the "Might of Islam".

There can be no gainsaying the fact that Persian chronicles are the major extant sources available to the historian of the Middle Ages, especially for the Delhi Sultanate. There are, however, other sources of information as well: epigraphy, numismatics, architecture, and a voluminous literature produced in the "courts" of the *ṣūfī* saints. With very few exceptions, these sources lack the coherence and chronology present in the chronicles, and they are, therefore, used as a repository of facts useful to substantiate or expand the material provided by the "histories". Information which contradicts the "evidence" of the court chronicles has frequently remained unexplored. The discourse of the monolithic state has therefore remained unquestioned.

It is, however, possible to pluck the seams in this discourse. The texts of the Persian court chronicles themselves are riddled with discrepancies, with niggling inconsistencies which are significant only if the reader approaches the text with the awareness that it carries information deliberately organised to impress specific conclusions upon the reader. These discrepancies in the text are important indicators of fractures in the discourse, dissonances which need to be enlarged with the aid of other source material. But giving space to the internal dissonances within a text is not always an easy task and it certainly does not contribute to the writing of monolithic, linear histories of state systems.

V. Political competition and the discourse of the unitary state

The premise of the unitary Muslim state, and a composite ruling elite owing allegiance to the Sultan of Delhi, would be difficult to question if we followed the obvious conclusions of the Persian chroniclers. Fakhr-i Mudabbir's *Ta'rīkh-i Fakhr al-Dīn Mubārak Shāh*, a text dedicated to Quṭb al-Dīn Ai-Beg, suggests, for example, that the favourite, competent military slave of Mu'izz al-Dīn, was appointed as the sole authority, the "viceroy" of his master's dominion in north India.

> This hero and world conqueror of Hind (Quṭb al-Dīn) was addressed as Malik,[28] and was made the heir apparent, *walī 'ahd*, to Hindustan, and the lands from the gates of Peshawar (Parshūr) to the limits of Hind were given to him, and the [authority] to appoint and remove, (literally, "unfasten and bind, *ḥall wa 'aqd*"), the remaining commanders was entrusted with him, *ba-dū mufauwaz gardānīd*. [Mu'izz al-Dīn] left [Quṭb al-Dīn] as his deputy and heir in the capital of Hindustan, *qā'im maqām wa walī 'ahd-i khud ba-dār al-mulk-i Hindustān ba-guzasht*, and sent him back to Delhi.[29]

The narrative of the near contemporary chronicler Minhāj-i Sirāj Jūzjānī also supported Quṭb al-Dīn's claims to be the *Amīr al-Umarā'*, the chief of the Mu'izzī military commanders in north India. Writing in the 660's/1260's for the Delhi Sultan Nāṣir al-Dīn (644-64/1246-66), Jūzjānī arranged his text to suggest that Delhi and its ruler had always been the paramount power in Hindustan.

Jūzjānī's narrative, however, was organised in the more disaggregated *ṭabaqāt* form, where each unit of the text studied "people belonging to one layer or class in the chronological succession of generations". As a result, his history moved beyond the sharp focus on the ruler and included accounts of social peers or dependents. Thus, the twentieth section, *ṭabāqa*, narrated the history of other important Mu'izzī subordinates in Hindustan without losing sight of his need to emphasise Quṭb al-Dīn's overall superiority.[30] In this section Jūzjānī provided a somewhat circumspect account of the independent ability of the Mu'izzī commanders to raise a military retinue, wage war, and sometimes compete with each other over the distribution of spoils. One such military commander was Bahā' al-Dīn Tughril, the governor of Thangir, in the province of Bayana.

According to Jūzjānī, Bahā' al-Dīn sought to improve the economy of his appanage by attracting merchants, *tujjar*, and well known men, *ma'arif-i rūy*, from different parts of Hindustan and Khurasan towards his domain. In an effort to encourage trade within the Bayana region, all merchants were granted accommodation and material support, *jumla-ra khāna wa asbāb mībakhshīd*, by the Mu'izzī subordinate. As a result, Jūzjānī noted, Bahā' al-Dīn Tughril made his province prosperous, an indication of which was the construction of Sulṭānkôt; a new capital to go with changed circumstances.[31] From Sulṭānkot, Bahā' al-Dīn commenced periodic raids towards Gwalior and was promised its territory by Mu'izz al-Dīn upon its capitulation. The seizure of Gwalior would have opened up the frontier into northern Rajasthan and Bundelkhand and brought considerable plunder and war material into the Amīr's reach. Bahā' al-Dīn's efforts to enlarge and consolidate his appanage were resisted by Quṭb al-Dīn Ai-Beg, who reacted to Bahā' al-Dīn's increasing influence in the area by seizing Gwalior himself in 597/1200. Jūzjānī, who narrated this incident, concluded rather diplomatically that as a result of the Gwalior episode there was (not?) a little dislike between Tughril and Quṭb al-Dīn, *miyān Malik...wa Sulṭān andak ghabārī būd*.[32]

Although Quṭb al-Dīn Ai-Beg may have believed and proclaimed that he was the supreme Mu'izzī commander in north India, his peers certainly did not share this opinion. Despite the predisposition of the Persian documentation towards Quṭb al-Dīn and the authority of Delhi, the presence of competing autonomous dominions could not be wholly obscured. Even the eulogy of the likes of Fakhr-i Mudabbir wore thin on occasion, and he confessed:

> And although all the victories which God caused him (Quṭb al-Dīn Ai-Beg) to win are clearer than the sun, and well known to all the world: nevertheless it must not be forgotten how much was due to the care and assistance of the *Sipahsālār* Ḥusām al-Dīn Aḥmad ʿAlī Shāh, who was the slave and officer of the King of Islām (Muʿizz al-Dīn), and was never absent from his stirrup, and was present at these victories and battles. Indeed all the generals of this court were gifted, brave and noble, and each was distinguished for his courage, and received an ample share of the fortune and prosperity of the King of Islam, who by his patronage and favour made each and all famous. To some he gave high commands, body guards, pavilions, drums, standards and districts, and each performed fine acts of service, and was duly praised...[33]

In a political world where all the generals of Mu'izz al-Dīn's court were "gifted, brave and noble, and each...received an ample share of the fortune and prosperity of the King of Islam, who...made each and all famous" there was also considerable rivalry and conflict. It is in the context of a fragmented political environment of the "north Indian Sultanates" (certainly in the plural), rather than a unitary dominion of the Delhi Sultanate, that we need to situate Quṭb al-Dīn Ai-Beg's urgency to appear as the unique *Amīr al-Umarā'*, the protector of the fortunes of the Muslim community.[34]

The construction of the Delhi *masjid-i jāmi'* was a part of Quṭb al-Dīn's effort to impress the Muslim congregation of his military and pious virtues. The inscriptions on the main entrance to the mosque remarked on his unique prowess and piety as a military commander destroying infidel temples. But again, given the nature of the political competition of the age, Quṭb al-Dīn was hardly unique in making statements of this nature. His rival in Bayana, Bahā' al-Dīn Tughril, also constructed congregational mosques which were architecturally similar in form and conception to the Delhi *masjid-i jāmi'*. The Bayana mosques also eulogised Bahā' al-Dīn as the conqueror of infidels and the creator of havens for Muslim congregations. But if Quṭb al-Dīn Ai-Beg's inscriptions in the Delhi *masjid-i jāmi'* drew the attention of the visitor to his military and moral accomplishments as the "viceroy" of Mu'izz al-Dīn Ghūrī, the visitor to the mosques in Bayana saw evidence of the same virtues in Bahā' al-Dīn's constructions. The only difference was that the inscriptions in the Bayana mosque went beyond Quṭb al-Din's claims and introduced Bahā' al-Dīn as *Pādishāh* and *Sulṭān*.[35]

Divorced from their assumed political context of a unitary dominion and a composite ruling elite, the discursive statements carried in texts like Delhi's *masjid-i jāmi'* need to be oriented to an audience other than that comprised of infidels. Indeed, the probity of the military commander as the paradigmatic Muslim leader, God's choice of a shepherd for his flock, was an important theme in the epigraphs in the mosque, but these statements seem to have been directed to the Muslims who visited the congregational mosques, and were aimed at displacing rival claims made by Mu'izzī peers.

VI. The congregational mosque and the "Hindus"

The Delhi *masjid-i jāmi'*, like other congregational mosques, differed from ordinary mosques in its size and function. Where the latter served the purpose of performing prayer for a limited number of people, the Delhi *masjid-i jāmi'* was a huge public monument created for the purposes of a congregational gathering of Muslims. Through the performance of prayer in congregation, Muslims acknowledged the fact that they were one united community who had submitted to the will of Allah. In the normal course of events, unbelievers, especially profane idolators, would not have been allowed within the precincts of the Delhi *masjid-i jāmi'* and, as a result they may have only possessed a general sense of the manner in which temple spoils were redeployed within the mosque. The architectural composition of the mosque, however, would have impressed the congregation of believers, who would have seen in it the evidence of their Amīr's ability to defeat infidels and provide a sanctuary for Islam.

Despite their ignorance of the precise architectural forms in the interior of the Delhi *masjid-i jāmi'*, it would be naive to assume that the "idolators" were unmoved by the destruction of their places of worship. But certainly within Delhi itself, there is no epigraphic record of rancour or sorrow at the destruction of temples, not even in the *devanagari* graffitis inscribed by Hindu artisans in the nooks and crannies of Quṭb al-Dīn's mosque.[36] Instead, one early inscription in a local dialect identifies the minaret as "the pillar of Malikdin. May it bring good fortune." Another anonymous artisan in 'Alā' al-Dīn's reign (695-715/1296-1316) had no hesitation in recognising the minaret as *Shrī Sultān Alāvadī Vijayasthamb*, the Sultan's pillar of victory. In Muḥammad Shāh Tughluq's reign (725-52/1325-51) the architects Nānā and Sālhā recorded their contribution to the repairs of the minaret in an inscription which also celebrated the completion of their work "by the grace of Sri Viśvakarmā".[37] Although the destruction, desecration, and appropriation of temple artifacts was an unexceptional event during conflict between rival Hindu kingdoms in the Middle Ages (and it is perfectly possible that Quṭb al-Dīn's conduct drew a reaction from the local population quite dissimilar from ours in a similar context), we need to nevertheless remember that the actions of the Mu'izzī commanders differed from those of the precedents set by the Hindu rulers.

Whereas Hindu rajas pillaged each other's temples, the authority of the vanquished lord was either appropriated or reconstituted within the temple shrine of the conqueror. The statements of conquest embodied in the process of destruction and reconstruction of imperial temples, was carried out within ritually homologous forms of Hindu kingship.[38] By contrast, Quṭb al-Dīn's statements of conquest in the *masjid-i jāmi'* redeployed temple spoils, but there was no sense of appropriation of authority. It signified instead the arrival of alternate traditions of governance in Delhi. This carried larger social and moral implications for the constitution of authority in Delhi since the royal temples were also the sites of redistributive and transactional relationships between the king, his subordinate chieftains and the larger subject population. Quṭb al-Dīn's conquest, destruction of temples and the construction of a mosque in their stead, fractured the relationship between the king and his subordinate chieftains. This development need not necessarily imply, however, a concomitant distancing of the subordinate echelon of rural chieftains from newly emerging structures of Sultanate authority. It is certainly worth querying whether the Mu'izzī governors constructed new, but different, relationships with these local political regimes in the countryside.[39]

The discourse of the Persian chronicles and the nature of the *masjid-i jāmi'* would suggest that this was not the case; political authority remained the exclusive preserve of the new Muslim Turkish elite and "Hindus" were hunted, not recruited, in the new political order. Stray references within the same chronicles, however, would suggest that this was hardly universally true. The author of an early Muslim epic of conquest, Fakhr-i Mudabbir, mentioned that *rātkān wa takrān/rautagān wa thakkurān*, petty ["Hindu"] chieftains and their military subordinates, were present within the ranks of the pillaging armies of Quṭb al-Dīn Ai-Beg.[40] We lack a sense of numbers and rôles occupied by these subordinates within the new dispensation, but their sheer presence forces us to reevaluate the relationships between the different ruling elites in ways more complicated than those suggested by a simple confessional divide.

The efforts of Quṭb al-Dīn, and other Mu'izzī commanders, towards consolidating relationships with "Hindu" chieftains only becomes clearer when we turn to other source material. In their ability to reach a far larger audience, the coinage of the Mu'izzī governors, even more than the *masjid-i jāmi'* in Delhi (or Bayana), served as effective discursive statements of conquest. Unlike the congregational mosque, however, the coinage carried statements of both conquest and reassurance to the conquered people. To begin with, the coins were unequivocal in their announcement of a new political order, and they introduced the new masters, the Mu'izzī *Amīrs*, as *Shrī Hammirah*; the Persian titles of the new lords stamped in the locally comprehensible *devanagari* script.

The presence of the new political order, however, did not seem to suggest any evidence of material change. The conquerors made no effort to alter the weight and purity of the precious metals in their coins which harmonised perfectly with existing circulating mediums. Deliberate attempts seem to have been made to emphasise continuity with the older patterns of fiscal and commercial exchange. Perhaps even more impressive was the confessional ambiguity in the sigilla of the Mu'izzī coins of this period. Emblems of a previous political regime, the image of God Shiva's vehicle, the *nandī* bull and the "Chauhan horseman" were stamped on the coins together with the title of *Shrī Hammirah*. Even more significant were the gold coins which carried both the outline of Lakshmī, the Hindu Goddess of wealth, and the Sultan's title in the *devanagari* script. As discursive statements, these coins made deliberate attempts to incorporate the conquered people within the newly established political and economic systems, not through pillage and mayhem, but through reassuring measures and symbols that suggested continuity with a preceding regime. These statements would suggest that "Muslim conquest" did not seek to traumatise the subject population and it certainly did not wish to create any major disjunctions in their material life. As the hoard evidence from north India confirms, Mu'izzī coins were valued as much as the earlier Rajput currencies and were fully assimilated within an economic world unimpressed with transitions in the political realm.[41]

Without devaluing the statement of plunder and conquest conveyed by the Delhi *masjid-i jāmi'*, it should not be forgotten that it is the Persian chronicles and the epigraphs in the mosque that make much of the episode of temple destruction. It is these texts which saw in the mosque the proof of the incumbent ruler's piety, a statement directed to the Muslim congregation in the mosque. From a different aspect, the destruction of the temple of the "Hindu" Raja was also necessary to break the social and political networks which sustained the old regimes. The ideology of iconoclasm, even within a "Hindu" context, carried the familiar sense of conquest and valour, but the construction of the *masjid-i jāmi'* denied a reconstitution of authority along old "familiar" lines. Within the new Sultanate regimes, "Hindu" subordinates might have been ritually distanced, but the sigilla on the coinage points to the presence of discourses – different "non-monumental" structures – which eased the political transition and sought to construct new, stable, productive relationships with the *rautagān wa thakkurān*. The trauma of the political change was assuaged somewhat by the remarkably restrained and confessionally ambiguous ways in which the new regime intruded into the life of a second rung of "Hindu" political commanders. Within the context of their own discursive statements, this was a fact that the Persian chronicles and the Delhi *masjid-i jāmi'* would not wish to recognise.

VII. Pietistic Muslim responses to the mosque

The main audience of the Delhi *masjid-i jāmi'* were the Muslim residents of the town. This community of Muslims increased in both size and heterogenous complexity during the 620s/1220s. Because of the destruction and havoc caused by the Mongol invasions, people from different regions in Afghanistan, eastern Iran, Transoxania and the central Asian steppes, immigrants of varied ethnic backgrounds, speaking distinct regional dialects, and with separate customary usages, made their way into what was, at that time, the sanctuary of north India. It is doubtful if they automatically felt any sense of solidarity with each other purely because they were denominationally Muslim. Many of them possessed artisanal skills which made a material difference to the regional economy of the fledgling Sultanate. Whether the presence of a greater number of "Muslims" contributed to any sense of an integrated community is a different question altogether. Jūzjānī's history was sensitive to the appearance of such large numbers of immigrants but, to his mind, integration was not a problem since the confessional solidarity of Islam overcame all distinctions between Muslims. Jūzjānī claimed that Iltutmish (607-33/1210-36) collected people from all parts of the world in Delhi,

> (which is) the capital of Hindustan, *dār al-mulk,* the centre of Islam, *dāira'i Islām*, the cradle of the commands and prohibitions of the *Sharī'at*, *mahbit-i awāmir wa nuwāhi-yi Sharī'at*, the keeper of the Muslim faith, *ḥauẓ-i dīn-i Muḥammadī*, the dais of the Muslim community, *manassa'i millat-i Aḥmadī*, the sanctuary of Islam in the eastern world, *Qubba'i Islām mashāriq-i gītī*...[42]

The author's description of Delhi as the *qubba'i Islām*, the sanctuary, the dome of Islam, conveyed to the reader the new identity of the capital in its axial role of representing the fortunes of the larger collectivity of Muslims. This was accurate enough in the context of Delhi's emerging military influence in north India; by 625/1228 Iltutmish had managed to defeat and annex the territories of the remnant Mu'izzī and Quṭbī commanders. Jūzjānī's representation of this political transformation, however, went much further. The chronicler's narrative suggested that just as Iltutmish's sultanate was a monolith, Islam was also a unitary, homogenous entity without any internal dissonances or complexities, at peace with itself, especially since the Delhi Sultan was its great protector.

Doubts about the degree of confessional coherence within the Muslim population of the Delhi Sultanate, however, emerge rather ironically from Jūzjānī's history itself. Towards the end of Iltutmish's reign, sometime around, or after 634/1236, Jūzjānī mentioned that a "sort" of learned man, *shakhṣī-yi dānishmand gūna,* by the name of Nūr Turk collected a large following near Delhi. According to the chronicler, this was a congregation of common people, *khalq-i 'awāmm*, who collected from distant areas like Gujarat, Sindh, the environs of Delhi and the banks of the Ganga and Jumna. They were strongly moved by Nūr Turk's exhortations, *taẓkīr*, where the preacher referred to the *'ulamā'* of the majority community, *'ulamā'i ahl-i sunnat wa jamā'at*, as those who had wronged the cause of ʿAlī. According to Jūzjānī, Nūr Turk specifically condemned the *'ulamā'* of the *Shāfi'ī* and *Ḥanafī* legal schools of interpretation, and instigated his followers to conspire against Islam, *qaṣd Islām kardand*. This group of people attacked the Delhi *masjid-i jāmi'*, an action which led Jūzjānī to describe the group as Shi'i Qarmatians and heretics, *mulāḥida wa qarāmiṭa*.[43]

Jūzjānī sought to obscure the significance of the "Muslim" attack on the Quṭb mosque by suggesting that it was the conspiracy of "heretics", a people who were outside the pale of the Sunni community. As a result, the attack on the *masjid-i jāmi'* would have remained one of the many curious details of a challenge which the "Muslim" sultanate had withstood successfully. A thorough vindication of the main protagonist in this story, however, by no less a person than the widely revered and respected *ṣūfī* saint Niẕām al-Dīn Awliyā', makes it impossible to accept Jūzjānī's gloss of the incident.

On the 13th of Shʿaban, 718/October 10, 1318, during one of his daily meetings with the congregation who visited his hospice in Delhi, the *ṣūfī* was queried about Nūr Turk and Jūzjānī's description of the derwish's beliefs and actions. Contrary to Jūzjānī's evaluation, Niẓām al-Dīn Awliyā' made it a point to clarify that Nūr Turk's faith was free from any heresy and absolved him of all Shīʿi *qarāmiṭa* links. According to Niẓām al-Dīn Awliyā', Nūr Turk had publicly criticised the *'ulamā'* because he had seen how polluted they had become by the material world of the capital, *ishān-rā āluda'i duniyā dīdī*. It was for this reason that the *'ulamā'* had fabricated all kinds of offensive charges (of the kind reported by Jūzjānī, no doubt) against the pious derwish, *u-rā badān chīzhā manṣūb kardand*.[44] In Niẓām al-Dīn Awliyā's recounting of the tale, Jūzjānī's appraisal of Nūr Turk coincided with the biased opinions of the *'ulamā'* in Delhi. The wheel had come full circle; for Niẓām al-Dīn Awliyā' it was the *sharī'a* minded *'ulamā'* who were not paragons of virtue or comportment.

The renewed discussion of Nūr Turk's beliefs, his animosity towards the Delhi *'ulamā'*, and Jūzjānī's account of the incident may well have cropped up accidentally during the course of Niẓām al-Dīn Awliyā's discourse. In the manner of his discussion of the Nūr Turk episode however, the *ṣūfī* saint's arguments did not merely rework Jūzjānī's report, it also sought to foreclose all options for independent analysis on this subject. If Nūr Turk's piety was unimpeachable, the conduct of the *'ulamā'* offensive, and Jūzjānī's history biased, then, without so much as actually articulating the thought, Niẓām al-Dīn Awliyā's narrative suggested that Nūr Turk's righteous moral indignation exonerated the derwish's attack on the *masjid-i jāmi'* and its corrupt *'ulamā'*. Hidden as a sub-text in this discussion was a comment on the sacred character of the Delhi *masjid-i jāmi'* if its *'ulamā'* misrepresented Islam.

These contrasting evaluations of Nūr Turk are important because they were made by two not entirely dissimilar people. Both Niẓām al-Dīn Awliyā' and Jūzjānī were members of the sunni-jama'a community, and both were popular preachers, respected for their piety. Yet, even within the sunni-jama'a community there were obviously wide differences in understanding the virtuous conduct of Muslims, especially amongst mystics and *sharī'a*-minded scholars. Some of these differences were explained by Niẓām al-Dīn Awliyā'.

> The *'ulamā'* are the people of intellect *ahl-i 'aql*, the derwishes are the people of love *ahl-i 'ishq*, the intellect of the *'ulamā'* overpowers, *ghālib*, [their sentiment] of love, [whereas] the [emotion] of [divine] love of these mystics triumphs over [their] intellect.[45]

Intellect in the thirteenth century, carried with it the associated meaning of a prescriptive, scholastic method of "knowing" a mortal's subordinate relationship with God. Conduct and belief for the individual Muslim was carefully worked out in its details in authoritative texts by the *'ulamā'*, with the intention of securing social conformity and the ideal of a unity within the Muslim community. This sharply reduced the opportunities for independent speculation, and contrasted with the emotion of divine love. In the *ṣūfī* understanding of Islam far greater importance was given to an inner, intuitive understanding of ritual. The faith of the believer could lead him to experience aspects of God's bounty and love, foreign to the cognition of the *'ulamā'*. As a result the *ṣūfī* could believe that "a preacher.... was so transported by his own eloquence that he flew away from the pulpit (*minbar*) to a neighbouring wall;...[that] meetings...[took place]...in deserted places with Khwājā Khizr who has everlasting life; ...[that there were] various 'fairy people' – ...*abdals* who physically fl[ew] above the territories which they protect from harm, ...[that] a holy man [circled] around the [*mihrāb* of the Delhi *masjid*] through the night till the dawn, ...[that] the *mardān-i ghaib*, men of the unseen, ...appear[ed] and disappear[ed], and sometimes call[ed] away a mortal to join them".[46] Whereas reason and intellect would regard these as patently fraudulent experiences, for many people in the early thirteenth century these were "real" events, evidence of God's intervention in an insecure mortal world. The mystic's interpretation of the individual's relationship with God resisted the authoritarian intervention of the intellect; the *nūr-i bātin* of the *ṣūfī*, his internal, hidden emotions, provided him with the space to contravene the *'ulamā's* understanding of the social dictates of the *sharī'a*.

This independence, the freedom to negotiate one's piety through a variety of prescriptive norms, was abhorrent to the *'ulamā'* who regarded the *ṣūfī* ability to mobilise huge congregations to their way of thinking as positively dangerous to the unity of Islam. The Delhi Sultans, nervous about the popular charismatic appeal of the saints, could not have agreed more with the conclusions of the *'ulamā'*. Although the Sultans lacked the ability of interfering and disciplining the conduct of the *ṣūfī*s, they could encourage a homogenity of conduct by constructing and patronising institutions which supported the *sharī'a*. Both Iltutmish and 'Alā' al-Dīn Khalajī, two sultans who added to and reconstructed the Quṭb mosque, took their rôles as the "preservers of the *sharīʿa* very seriously. ʿAlā' al-Dīn's inscription in the mosque explained the Delhi Sultan's contribution:

> When God Almighty, whose greatness is sublime and whose names are exalted, for the revival of the laws of the [Muslim] community, *ihyā'yi marāsim-i millat*,[47] and the elevation of the banners of the *sharīʿat*, chose the lord of the Caliphs of the world, *khudaygān-i Khulafā'i jahānrā*, so that every moment the foundations of the Muslim religion, *asās-i dīn-i Muḥammadī*, and the roots, *binā-yi*, of the Muslim *sharīʿa* are strengthening, *istiḥkām mīpazīrad/qawī mīgardad*, and for preserving the state and consolidating the Sultanate, *dawām-i mamlikat wa niẓām-i Sulṭanat*, [the lord of the Caliphs] built mosques in accordance with the commands of Him beside whom there is no God, (*Qur'ān* IX: 18) "But he only shall visit the mosques who believes in God".[48]

Other than acknowledging the divine dispensation of authority to ʿAlā' al-Dīn, the Khalajī inscriptions linked "reviving", "protecting" and "strengthening" the *sharīʿa* to the construction of mosques. ʿAlā' al-Dīn's constructions created the material conditions in which Muslims could cleanse themselves of sin, and it is for this reason that another inscription implored: "may God perpetuate his kingdom (so that he may continue) to build mosques, and preserve till eternity his sovereignty (so as to protect) the lustre of the places of worship".[49]

Iltutmish's inscriptions quoted the *Qur'ān, sūra* 62: 9-10, to clarify the importance of performing the obligatory rituals of prayer in the midst of one's daily activity:

> O' believers, when proclamation is made for prayer on Friday, hasten to God's remembrance and leave trafficking aside; that is better for you, did you but know. Then when the prayer is finished, scatter in the land and seek God's bounty, and remember God frequently; haply you will prosper.[50]

Another inscription cited the traditions of the Prophet Muḥammad to emphasise the connections between individual and congregational worship.

> The Prophet....said, "whoever offered his morning prayer in congregation got his (worldly) troubles removed by Allah; and whoever offered his afternoon prayer (in congregation) got his living made plentiful by Allah; and whoever offered his late afternoon prayer (in congregation) became (as pure) as on the day he was born; and whoever offered his evening prayer in congregation is considered as if he has given away his wealth and (even) his life (in the way of Allah), and whoever offered his bed-time prayer in congregation received Allah's blessing". (The Prophet)...said, "whoever observed these five prayers in congregation would have his way (to Heaven) widened by Allah."[51]

As a part of their "administrative" repertory aimed at controlling their Muslim subjects, the Delhi Sultans needed the *'ulamā'* in their supervisory rôle of enforcing obedience to the *sharī'a*. The construction of mosques and schools proclaimed the Sultan's pietistic intentions while providing the *'ulamā'* with the monumental sites where the Muslims could be socialised into following the prescriptive codes of the *sharī'a*. It was the socially fragmented world of the Muslims that the Delhi Sultans sought to cohere within one community, governed by one law, under the authority of a morally upright monarch. The Delhi *masjid-i jāmi'* was extremely important in disseminating this sentiment, and 'Alā' al-Dīn Khalajī was very direct in developing its sacred significance. His inscription on the left pier of the south door to the mosque argued:

> he ('Alā' al-Dīn) built this mosque, which is the mosque of paradise, for saints and....men of piety and a place of assembly of the eminent angels, and an edifice inhabited by the souls of the chief prophets.[52]

'Alā' al-Dīn did not question the spiritual authority of the saints of God, *awliyā'*, instead he argued that together with angels and prophets, their presence in his *masjid-i jāmi'* was on account of the sacredness of the mosque. It was the Delhi Sultan's special relationship with God and His blessings which had transformed the mosque into a hallowed precinct. Rather than the congregation lending significance to the mosque, the pious congregated in the *masjid* because of its holy character and accepted the dictates of the *sharīʿa* which it represented.

As we have already seen, Nūr Turk was far from impressed by similar claims made by Iltutmish. Although he had chosen a more direct military recourse in challenging the *Sharīʿatī* order constructed by the Delhi Sultan, Niẓām al-Dīn relied upon his teachings to counter the coercion of the *ʿulamā'*. In establishing an alternative disciplinary formation, the teachings of the *ṣūfī* were as threatening to Sultanate "order" as an armed attack. There was no mincing of words in his inversion of ʿAlā' al-Dīn's claims regarding the sacredness of the Delhi *masjid-i jāmiʿ*:

> [Niẓām al-Dīn] asserted: "Whatever place there might be, it is scented by the blessed feet [of the *ṣūfī* saints]. Take, for example, the Delhi *masjid-i jāmiʿ*. The feet of so many saints and pious have trod there, which is why that place has so much tranquility."[53]

In other words, ʿAlā' al-Dīn's *masjid-i jāmiʿ* would have remained a spiritless place, a pile of stones and mortar, had the *ṣūfī* saints not transformed it. It was important to make this point in case visitors to the mosque attributed the pious environment of the mosque to its constructors, the Delhi Sultans. Niẓām al-Dīn wanted to make sure that his audience realised that the "tranquility" of the place originated from the blessings of the saints of God and not from the efforts of the Delhi Sultans.

VIII. Conclusion:
"Objective" history and the memory of the Quṭb

At the time of its construction, the Delhi *masjid-i jāmiʿ* left a variety of different impressions upon visitors. For many it was a symbol of a flourishing Muslim community abiding by the tenets of the *sharīʿa*, triumphant over its idolatorous opponents, secured by the energetic, armed interventions of its Sultans. For others, it was a haven for "scholars", who were concerned less with the spiritual fate of their congregations and more with a coercive regimen of rituals, pecuniary gains and their own authority. These claims and counter claims were very much a part of the history of Delhi's first *masjid-i jāmi'* in the thirteenth and fourteenth centuries. Events after the thirteenth century consolidated rival interpretations of the congregational mosque and the modern memory of the Quṭb was strongly impressed with these conflicting images.

For over three centuries after 'Alā' al-Dīn Khalajī's death (715/1316), the old *masjid-i jāmi'* was sporadically associated with the authority of the rulers of Delhi. But this was not at the expense of the *ṣūfī*s whose influence remained undiminished during this period. In the fourteenth century itself, the tomb of Niẓām al-Dīn Awliyā' emerged as the most venerated shrine in the region of Delhi, completely eclipsing the Delhi *masjid-i jāmi'*. The area around his shrine was blessed by the grace of the saint and his disciples chose to be buried in the proximity of their *pīr*, their intercessor with God at the day of judgement. Amongst many others buried in this necropolis was the Mughal emperor Humāyūn (died 963/1556), and a pilgrimage to the *dargāh*, or the "court" of Niẓām al-Dīn Awliyā', was a part of the Mughal itinerary whenever the rulers of the dynasty visited Delhi.[54] Mughal patronage to the shrine, paradoxically, "controlled" the discourse of the saint against the inadequacies of temporal government. The Mughals did not hesitate to appear as disciples of mystic saints and incorporated strains of mysticism within an ideological baggage explaining their rites of kingship.

The example of Niẓām al-Dīn Awliyā' notwithstanding, not all *ṣūfī* shrines were equally hegemonised by the Mughals. To the south of Delhi, near the old *masjid-i jāmi'*, the *dargāh* of Quṭb al-Dīn Bakhtiyār Kākī (died 634/1236) was also an important *ṣūfī* shrine. Although he was not an unusually influential saint in his own life time, Bakhtiyār Kākī was the *pīr* of Bābā Farīd, Niẓām al-Dīn Awliyā's spiritual master, and the renown of the student had certainly accrued to his teachers as well.[55] The record of royal visitations to the *dargāh* suggests that Bakhtiyār Kākī's shrine emerged as a pilgrimage site as early as the late fourteenth and early fifteenth centuries.[56] In 932/1526 it was included in Babar's tour of significant areas worthy of visitation in Delhi and in the mid 1150s/early 1740s Dargāh Qulī Khān commenced his account of Delhi's *ṣūfī* shrines with a narration of Bakhtiyār Kākī's *dargāh*.[57] Bakhtiyār Kākī may have lacked the popularity of Niẓām al-Dīn Awliyā', but in the eighteenth and nineteenth centuries, his mystical powers were considered commanding enough that the Mughal emperors Shāh 'Ālam Bahādur Shāh (1119-24/1707-12), Jalāl al-Dīn Shāh 'Ālam (1173-1221/1760-1806) and Mu'īn al-Dīn Akbar (1221-53/1806-1837) chose to be buried near the *dargāh*. The wish of the last Mughal ruler, Bahādur Shāh "Ẓafar" (1253-74/1837-58), to be buried near the saint remained unfulfilled; he was deported to Rangoon by the British where he died.[58]

Unlike Niẓām al-Dīn's *dargāh*, Bakhtiyār Kākī's charisma did not materially alter the prestige of the Mughal emperors. This was not because of any shortcoming in the saint's popularity. By the end of the eighteenth century, Mughal might had not survived the onslaught of the Afghan, Maratha and British incursions and its capacity to command obedience was in obvious decline. The Mughal ability to access the increasing popularity of Bakhtiyār Kākī's shrine for its own ends was also severely limited. In the eighteenth century many people in Delhi regarded Quṭb al-Dīn Bakhtiyār Kākī as the seniormost in the "hierarchy of saints", the *Quṭb al-aqṭāb*, specially chosen by God to maintain order in the world. The actual extent of his influence is uncertain, but at least within a local, popular cosmology evident in Delhi in the late eighteenth, early nineteenth century, Bakhtiyār Kākī was regarded as the *Quṭb*, the axis, around whom the world revolved. This interpretation was also provided an iconic representation when the *mīnār* of the neighbouring, thirteenth century *masjid-i jāmi'*, was described as *Quṭb ṣāhib kī lāth*. In other words, the minaret was believed to represent the staff of Quṭb al-Dīn Bakhtiyār Kākī which pierced the sky, and like the *pīr* himself, connected heaven with earth, providing stability and shelter to mortals on earth.[59] In this reworked popular cosmology, it was the saint who was the *qubbat al-Islām*, the "sanctuary of Islam" and not the congregational mosque. It was in acknowledgement of the *pīr's* charisma, that the minaret of the mosque was christened the Quṭb mīnār, the name which it still carries today.

The reason why we have any information at all about the later developments in the meaning of the *masjid-i jāmi'* is because of attempts made in the nineteenth and twentieth centuries to correct some of these "errors". In 1263/1846-7 the *munṣif*, judge, employed with the British East India Company, Sayyid Ahmad Khan, wrote his famous topographical monograph on Delhi, the *Āṣār al-Sanādīd*. At that stage in his life, Sayyid Ahmad was strongly influenced by the emerging positivistic historiographical methodologies gaining currency in the west. In his research on Delhi's monuments, the scholar was extremely careful in citing his literary and archaeological evidence, and in ascertaining chronological, geographical and lexicographical details. Subsequent to the *Āṣār al-Sanādīd*, Sayyid Ahmad Khan published critical editions of Abū' al-Faẓl's *Ā'īn-i Akbarī*, Ẓiyā' al-Dīn Baranī' *Ta'rīkh-i Fīrūz Shāhī*, and Jahāngīr's, *Tūzuk-i Jahāngīrī*, all medieval Persian chronicles on which he had started work several years ago. The course of his research was charted by his belief that "only a correct and sober presentation of the facts can convey a true sense of direction in history and enable the Indians to arrive at a realistic assessment of their situation".[60] The documentary record of the court chronicles was an important source for the historian, and Sayyid Ahmad Khan carefully selected texts which were, in his opinion, repositories of reliable, objective information.

His concern to recount the "correct facts" about the capital of the great Sultans and the Mughals motivated Sayyid Ahmad Khan to write the most comprehensive text on the monuments of Delhi. In his account of Delhi's old congregational mosque, he did mention that one of the names for the minaret was "*Quṭb ṣāhib kī lāth*", and, amongst other names, the *masjid* was also called *Quwwat al-Islām*.[61]

Presumably, because these names belonged to the realm of an oral, popular culture, and not to an "objective", "scientific", verifiable, documentary record, there was no discussion of why the mosque and the *mīnār* were ascribed such intriguing names. Sayyid Ahmad Khan's text led the reader away from these names towards the more "relevant" subject of the architectural and epigraphical content of the monument and each Sultan's contribution to its construction.

In its own turn, the *Āṣār al-Sanādīd* was regarded as an "authoritative" text because it carried all the evidence of sound historical research. Archaeologists and historians of a later generation were dependent upon Sayyid Ahmad Khan's collection of data, his readings of the epigraphs, bibliography of sources, and discussion of the authorship and architectural significance of the mosque. The major development in the early twentieth century occured when the analysis of the congregational mosque was further elaborated by an emerging consensus about the history of the Delhi Sultanate. Ironically, in their research in this area as well, scholars continued to be dependent upon Sayyid Ahmad Khan's scholarship. It was his editions of the Persian chronicles which became the staple diet for most medievalists, because their "factual account[s]", scholars in the twentieth century noted, were "correct in all substantive matters".

There is no doubt that the scholarship on the medieval period today bears little resemblance to that of Sayyid Ahmad's time. Irfan Habib's work in itself has inspired research into questions concerning material culture, agricultural production and the structures of the state. These developments notwithstanding, historians are still wary of examining medieval Persian texts as discursive constructions of evidence, as images which sought to shape reality. In the absence of such interrogation, a circular logic which first locates "authoritative" sources, and then reconstructs a "definitive" history of the Middle Ages, has led to the writing of histories which have in different ways remained congruent with the fortunes of the state.

This methodology has left little space for the presence of local histories, popular memories or contesting discourses in the history of medieval India.[62] For the Quṭb mosque, it led to the "clarification" that the minaret was not named after the *ṣūfī* saint Quṭb al-Dīn Ba<u>kh</u>tiyār Kākī, but the military commander Quṭb al-Dīn Ai-Beg. The term *Qubbat al-Islām*, or the "Sanctuary of Islam", which was at first ambiguously used by Jūzjānī for Iltutmish's Delhi and later applied to define the spiritual domain of Ba<u>kh</u>tiyār Kākī, was transformed into *Quwwat al-Islām*, or the "Might of Islam" and used for Quṭb al-Dīn's mosque. This name coincided more closely with the military persona of the first constructor of the mosque and his proclamation of a new political order built out of the rubble of temples. Despite all the other developments in research on medieval Indian history, this interpretation of the mosque has remained unquestioned. In that sense, the problem before us today is not a simple one of reinterpreting the significance of the Quṭb monuments. We need to be aware that it is the epistemologies dominant in the study of medieval Indian history that enable the interpretation of the Quṭb monuments as the "*Quwwat al-Islām*" mosque.

As purveyors of "information", historians shape the contours of India's past, in history text-books, school and college syllabi and the popular media. Despite the best intentions of many of these practitioners, their work only serves to consolidate popular misconceptions concerning the monolithic character of Hindu and Muslim social structures in the medieval period. Historians may no longer use the term "Muslim period" to refer to the subcontinent's Middle Ages, but their histories still consider the Delhi Sultans and the Mughal *padshāhs* as the principal actors in the history of medieval India. The different rulers and their structures of administration, revenue and diplomatic policies are studied as the agencies which introduced social and economic change in the subcontinent. Marxist analyses of relations of exploitation and dominance in Sultanate and Mughal society, confirm the image of a monolithic ruling elite, predominantly Muslim and obsessed with "a" Persian culture. This static and undifferentiated account is disturbed only occasionally by the *bhaktī*, sometimes the *ṣūfī*, perhaps even by groups such as the Mahdawīs. But these are often discussed as dissenting groups, "non-conformist movements", related to, but outside the pale of two well contoured religions. During this entire period "Muslims" remained the politically dominant group within the subcontinent. The relationship of these historiographies and the memory of the Quṭb is extremely important. The events and individuals – Quṭb al-Dīn Ai-Beg or Quṭb al-Dīn Ba<u>kh</u>tiyār Kākī, for example – are not terribly significant in themselves, but once situated within larger contextual frames of signification they recall a host of memories. The Quṭb is one of those historic sites which can extend beyond its own historical moment to carry a much larger symbolic statement.

Part of its importance lies in the manner in which it has been preserved and "done up" into a national and world heritage monument. In one of its advertisement campaigns the *Hindustan Times,* a national newspaper, asked its readers the rhetorical question: "Can you imagine Delhi without the Qutb?" Its ruins are presented today as a part of "Indian" antiquity, a part of each citizen's inheritance which he or she can cherish. One mosque out of several from the twelfth century has gained this doubtful honour. Indians are asked to take pride in "their" *mīnār* – we are told that it is one of the tallest free standing minarets built out of stone and mortar. Nationalist pride, however, is shortlived and the Quṭb monuments lead to a host of ambivalent reactions.

If the minaret is wonderful, what of the mosque? Responses vary. For many, especially children, the monument is an incredibly beautiful and grandiose palace or a large congregational hall. That it is a mosque escapes most of them. Other, more "discerning" visitors, remain disconcerted by the statues, pillars, and elaborate carvings, so obviously of a Hindu/Jain provenance situated within a congregational mosque. Still others may see in the mosque evidence of the might and dominance of "their community" in the affairs of the subcontinent in the near past.

Since it is a major tourist site, the Archaeological Survey of India has placed short descriptions inscribed on stone near the several monuments to "guide" visitors through the Quṭb complex. These inscriptions provide the name, the physical properties, functions and significance of the respective monuments. These are facts; there is no hint of doubt, speculation or debate concerning the multiple interpretations of these sites or the changing historical contexts in which they were built. Instead, the self-confident recounting of undisputed information is in itself reassuring to the visitors. It is presented as the consensual wisdom of a professional body of historians and archaeologists, the "authorities" whose knowledge should be above doubt.

Once armed with the crucial information that the *Quwwat al-Islām masjid* celebrates the conquest of Hindustan by the Muslim Sultans of Delhi the nature of the monument itself leaves little space to visitors for doubt. Even as they function as historians themselves, the "evidence" of plunder before them is "proof" sufficient of Muslim iconoclasm and a bigoted hatred of Hindus and their religious beliefs. Their empirical conclusions are not very far from a seamless historiography of medieval Indian history which has provided little to contest the overriding impression of the hegemony of the Muslim state.[63] As a result, the Quṭb serves as a catalyst which resurrects a host of memories about Muslims and their governance: from casual stories concerning Muslim fanaticism and violence, to history lessons where Muslim rulers and their subordinates monopolised power and exploited Hindu subjects. Within the mosque the visitor is struck by the juxtaposition of the great monolithic communities, a divide which the Quṭb suggests commenced from the very intrusion of Islam into India. A partition which from its very first encounter was remarkable for its violence.

More than any large tome or pedagogical instruction, the Quṭb provides an opportunity to educate visitors about the complex fragmented political and religious world of India's Middle Ages, a time when there was considerable disunity and contestation within the groups defined as "Hindus" and "Muslims". It is this frame of reference which should also guide us to reflect upon the manner in which discursive constructions of knowledge were formed in the Middle Ages. The *Qubbat al-Islam* mosque was built to represent a unity of belief and conduct to a Muslim congregation who not only remained quite unimpressed with Sultanate statements of piety and power but also produced their own contesting discursive texts. The spoils of the Hindu and Jain temples are only a small part of the story of the Quṭb; Mu'izzī *amīrs* such as Bahā' al-Dīn Tug͟hril, *ṣūfī* derwishes like Nūr Turk, *shaykhs* like Niẓām al-Dīn Awliyā', the popular veneration of Quṭb al-Dīn Ba͟khtiyār Kākī and the historiography of Sayyid Ahmad Khan and his successors are all ingredients that should be used to explain the multi-leveled history of the mosque and minaret to visitors. Instead it is the extreme nationalist ideologies prevalent in India which filter our understanding of the Quṭb. This unfortunately also burdens visitors with unequivocal evidence of wrongs inflicted in the past upon the Hindu community, wrongs that are in need of correction today. As a result, the Quṭb stands as an icon, encapsulating the trauma of 1947 and acting as a historical exoneration for the acts of December 1992. What is tragic is the manner in which historians of medieval India have provided "proof" and "evidence" supporting the readings of this icon.

Notes

1 This is an abbreviated version of a paper presented at the Indo-French Seminar (sponsored by the UGC, ICHR and the Maison des Sciences de l'Homme) held at the School of Social Sciences, Jawaharlal Nehru University, 14–16 February, 1994. A revised version of this paper is included in my forthcoming book titled 'Sites of Power and Resistance: A Study of Sultanate Monumental Architecture'. The paper has profited

from the comments of Anjali Kumar, David Gilmartin, Dilip Menon, Ebba Koch, Gail Minault, Suvir Kaul and Tanika Sarkar, none of whom necessarily share the opinions of the author expressed here.

2 Alfred Gell, "The Technology of Enchantment and the Enchantment of Technology", in *Anthropology, Art and Aesthetics*, ed. J. Coote and Anthony Shelton (London: Oxford University Press, 1992), pp.40–63.

3 For details on the spatial, architectural and epigraphic information, other than my own field surveys, I am reliant on the research of Sayyid Ahmad Khan, Alexander Cunningham, J. Horowitz, J.A. Page, A.B.M. Husain, M.A. Husain, and Ebba Koch. The full bibliographical citations are given below.

4 Although there is absolutely no evidence to warrant such an assumption all historians and archaeologists have concluded that it was the Muslims who placed the iron pillar within the Quṭb mosque. Their conclusions might have been guided by the fact that later rulers like Fīrūz Shāh Tughluq and Akbar transported Asokan pillars and placed them as trophies in Delhi and Allahabad respectively. As Richard H. Davis, "Indian Art Objects as Loot", *Journal of Asian Studies*, 52 (1993): 22–48, has pointed out, however, temples were also plundered by Hindu rulers, and their idols were frequently treated as war trophies and publicly displayed as statements of conquest. A similar effort at embellishing his own authority may well have guided the Tomara ruler Anangpal sometime around 1052. At least according to popular legends, it was this ruler who placed the fourth century iron pillar at its current site. See Alexander Cunningham, "Four Reports made during the years 1862-63-64-65", *Archaeological Survey of India Reports* (Simla: Archaeological Survey of India, Government Press, 1871), vol. 1, pp.171–175.

5 See, for example, the opinion of H.C. Fanshawe, *Shah Jahan's Delhi – Past and Present* (Delhi: Sumit Publications, 1979 reprint of 1902 edition), p.257.

6 See Sayyid Ahmad Khan, *Āṣār al-Sanādīd* ed. Khaliq Anjum (Delhi: Urdu Academy Delhi, 1990 reprint of 1847 edition), Alexander Cunningham, "Four Reports...", J. Horowitz, "The Inscriptions of Muhammad ibn Sam, Qutbuddin Aibeg and Iltutmish", *Epigraphia Indo-Moslemica* (1911-12): 12–34, J. Yazdani, "Inscriptions of the Khaljī Sultans of Delhi and their contemporaries in Bengal" *Epigraphia Indo-Moslemica* (1917-18), pp.23–30, J.A. Page, *A Historical Memoir*

on the Qutb (Calcutta: Memoirs of the Archaeological Survey of India, no. 22, Government of India Central Publication Branch, 1926).

7 As far as I have been able to date it, Sayyid Ahmad Khan was the first author to refer to the Delhi *masjid-i jāmi‘* as the *"Quwwat al-Islām"* mosque. S.A. Khan, *Āṣār al-Sanādīd*, vol. 1, p.310, provided three names for the mosque: *Masjid-i Adīna Dehlī yā* (or) *Masjid-i Jāmi‘ Dehlī yā* (or) *Quwwat al-Islām*. Cunningham (1871) either misread *Quwwat al-Islām* in Khan's text as *Quṭb al-Islām* or, as is more likely (see below), he relied upon a locally current source for his reading. Literature on Delhi produced for English tourists at the turn of the century always referred to the mosque as *Quwwat al-Islām*. See H.C. Fanshawe, *Delhi – Past and Present*, p.258, and Gordon Risley Hearn, *The Seven Cities of Delhi* (New Delhi: SBW Publishers, 1986 reprint of 1906 edition), pp.51, 54, 94. Some years later, the widely cited Horowitz, "Inscriptions..." *Epigraphia Indo-Moslemica* (1911-12) and J.A. Page, *Qutub...*, (1926), informed scholars that *Quwwat al-Islām* was the name of this mosque. It was a fateful christening for it was to eventually become the "official" name of the mosque. From two edges of the historiographical spectrum where this term is used for the *masjid-i jāmi‘*, see: J. Burton Page, "Dihli", *Encyclopaedia of Islam*, ed. C.E. Bosworth et al. (Leiden: E.J. Brill, second edition, 1956), vol. 2, pp.255–266, representing the "Islamicist" tradition, and Y.D. Sharma, *Delhi and it Neighbourhood* (New Delhi: Director General Archaeological Survey of India, 1982 reprint), pp.17–19, 52–9, amongst the better tourist guide literature.

8 Michael W. Meister, "The Two-and-a-half day Mosque", *Oriental Art* 18 n.s. (1972): 57–63; Mohammad Mujeeb, "The Qutb Complex as a Social Document", in *Islamic influence on Indian Society* (Delhi: Meenakshi Prakashan, 1972), pp.114–127; and A.B.M. Husain, *The Manara in Indo-Muslim Architecture*, (Dacca: Asiatic Society of Pakistan, Publication no. 25, 1970).

9 Robert Hillenbrand, "Political Symbolism in Early Indo-Islamic Mosque Architecture: the Case of Ajmīr", *Iran* 26 (1988): 105–117. Anthony Welch, "Architectural Patronage and the Past: The Tughluq Sultans of India", *Muqarnas* 10 (1993): 311–322.

10 Welch, "Architectural Patronage...", p.314.

11 Anthony Welch, "*Qur'ān* and Tomb: the Religious Epigraphs of two early Sultanate Tombs in Delhi" in *Indian Epigraphy: its bearings on the History of Art*, ed. Frederick M. Asher and G.S. Ghai (New Delhi: Oxford and IBH Publishing Co., American Institute of Indian

Studies, 1985), pp.260, 257. Welch summarised here arguments which he presented in another, apparently still unpublished article: "Islamic Architecture and Epigraphs in Sultanate India" in *Studies in South Asian Art and Architecture*, ed. A.K. Narain, forthcoming.

12 Ibid., p.257.

13 In Welch's analysis, "Architectural Patronage...", pp.311, 312, 313, 314: "Building types – mosques, tombs, madrasas, and minars – as well as forms are also at the same time assertively alien to the Hindu majority, and in their strident distinctiveness from indigenous buildings, they proclaim Islam's universal aspirations and its distance from the polytheism of the subject population" (pp.312-3).

14 A.B.M. Habibullah, *The Foundation of Muslim Rule in India*, (Allahabad: Central Book Depot, 1976 reprint), Khaliq Ahmad Nizami, *Some Aspects of Religion and Politics in the Thirteenth Century*, (Delhi: Idarah-i Adabiyat-i Delli, 1974 reprint), S.B.P. Nigam, *Nobility under the Sultans of Delhi, A.D. 1206–1398* (Delhi: Munshiram Manoharlal, 1968).

15 Habibullah, *Foundation of Muslim Rule*, ch. VI, pp.120–134.

16 Welch, "Architectural Patronage...", p.311.

17 "The plebianization of the nobility", a clumsy formulation at best, has several proponents but was first suggested by Mohammad Habib, "The Governing Class" in *The Political Theory of the Delhi Sultanate* (Allahabad: Kitab Mahal, n.d.), pp.144–151, and later developed by Irfan Habib, "Barani's Theory of the Delhi Sultanate", *Indian Historical Review* 7 (1980-81), p.109.

18 For the architectural consequences of this development see Welch, "Architectural Patronage and the Past", pp.314-5. Here the author argues that since the Tughluqs were [more?] secular rulers, governing a pan-Indian state, their architecture was also less "saracenic" and more eclectic.

19 Irfan Habib, "The Social distribution of Landed Property in pre-British India (a Historical Survey)", *Enquiry* n.s. 2 (1965), p.45.

20 Irfan Habib, *The Agrarian System of Mughal India* (Bombay: Asia Publishing House, 1963), p.257.

21 Tapan Raychaudhry, "The State and the Economy" in *The Cambridge Economic History of India*, ed. Tapan Raychaudhuri and Irfan Habib (Cambridge: University Press, 1982), vol. 1, p. 184.

22 Ibid.

23 Habibullah, *Foundation of Muslim Rule*, ch. V-VI, pp.96–134, Habib, *Agrarian System of Mughal India*, p.318.

24 Irfan Habib, "The Price Regulations of 'Alā'uddīn Khaljī — A defence of Ẓiā' Baranī" *Indian Economic and Social History Review* 21 (1984), p.393.

25 Shireen Moosvi, *The Economy of the Mughal Empire, c. 1595: A Statistical Study* (Delhi: Oxford University Press, 1987), p.4.

26 Irfan Habib, "Evidence for Sixteenth century Agrarian Conditions in the Guru Granth Sahib" *Indian Economic and Social History Review* 1 (1963-64), p.70.

27 Athar Ali, "The Mughal Polity – a Critique of 'Revisionist' Approaches", *Proceedings of the Indian History Congress* 52 (1991-2), pp.308, 310.

28 *"īn pahwān (?) wa jahāndār-i Hind-ra Malik khitāb farmūd"*. *"Pahwān"* in the Persian edition of the *Ta'rīkh* must be a mistake for *"pahalwān"*.

29 Fakhr-i Mudabbir, *Ta'rīkh-i Fakhr al-Dīn Mubārak Shāh*, ed. E.D. Ross (London: Royal Asiatic Society, 1927), pp.28-9.

30 On the *ṭabaqāt* form as a historical genre of writing see Franz Rosenthal, *History of Muslim Historiography*, (Leiden: E.J. Brill, 1969), pp.93–95 and Louise Marlow, *Hierarchy and Egalitarianism in Islamic Thought* (Cambridge: University Press, 1997), pp.9-10. For the Mu'izzī subordinates in Hindustan, see Minhāj-i Sirāj Jūzjānī, *Ṭabaqāt-i Nāṣirī*, ed. Abdul Hayy Habibi, (Kabul: Anjuman-i Tarikh-i Afghanistan, 1963-4), vol. 1, pp.415–438.

31 Jūzjānī, *Ṭabaqāt...*, vol. 1, p.421.

32 Ibid, vol. 1, p.421. Notice also the titulature and Jūzjānī's attempt to communicate his sense of the heirarchical relationship: Malik was used for Bahā' al-Dīn and Sultan for Quṭb al-Dīn.

33 Fakhr-i Mudabbir, *Ta'rīkh-i Fakhr al-Dīn Mubārak Shāh*, pp.25-6. I have used the translation of E.D. Ross, "The genealogies of Fakhr al-Din Mubarak Shah" in *'Ajab Namah: A Volume of Oriental Studies presented to E.G. Browne on his 60th birthday*, ed. T.W. Arnold and R.A. Nicholson (Cambridge: University Press, 1922), p.399;

34 For a more detailed treatment of the evidence and argument see my *The Emergence of the Delhi Sultanate* (Delhi: Permanent Black, 2007).

35 For Bahā' al-Dīn's inscription in the "Chaurasi Khamba" mosque in Kaman, see Mehrdad and Natalie H. Shokoohy, "The architecture

of Baha al-Din Tughrul (sic) in the region of Bayana, Rajasthan", *Muqarnas* 4 (1987), p.115.

36 But note the graffiti on the right-hand jamb of the eleventh slit window on the stairway in the minaret: "May your mother be ravished by a donkey!" See Page, *The Qutb...*, p.40. This may have been a response to the destruction of temples, but at least equally, if not more likely, a venting of frustrated resentment by an artisan at a personal injury caused by an aggressive supervisor at work.

37 See Page, *The Qutb...*, pp.39-40, 41, 43. I have followed the revised and edited translations of Pushpa Prasad, *Sanskrit Inscriptions of Delhi Sultanate 1191–1526* (Delhi: Oxford University Press, 1990), pp.3, 19, 35. I concur with Pushpa Prasad's reading of the inscription from Muḥammad Shāh Tug͟hluq's reign. But for an alternate reading see Carl W. Ernst, *Eternal Garden; Mysticism, History and Politics at a South Asian Sufi Center* (Albany: State University of New York, 1992), pp.32-3.

38 See Davis, "Indian Art Objects as Loot", pp.22–48.

39 Peter Hardy, "Growth of Authority over a Conquered Political Elite: Early Delhi Sultanate as a Possible Case Study" in *Kingship and Authority in South Asia*, ed. J.F. Richards (Delhi: Oxford University Press, 1998 reprint), pp.216–241, had studied a similar set of questions years ago without much success. Significantly his research was based primarily on the textual evidence of the thirteenth and fourteenth centuries.

40 Fak͟hr-i Mudabbir, *Ta'rīk͟h...*, p.33, Hardy, "Authority over a Conquered Political Elite", p.238.

41 See John S. Deyell, *Living without Silver* (Delhi: Oxford University Press, 1990), pp.193–206, 318.

42 Jūzjānī, *Ṭabaqāt....*, vol. 1, pp.440-1.

43 Jūzjānī, *Ṭabaqāt...*, vol. 1, p.461.

44 Amīr Ḥasan Sijzī, *Fawā'id al-Fu'ād*, ed. Khwaja Hasan Sani Nizami (Delhi: Urdu Academy, 1990), p.334.

45 Sijzī, *Fawā'id al-Fu'ād*, p.226.

46 Simon Digby, "The Sufi Shaikh as a source of authority in Medieval India", *Purusartha, Islam et Societe en Asie du Sud* 9 (1986), p.62.

47 The picture of the Delhi Sultan as the "reviver of the forgotten commandments, *muhaī'yī āṣār-i aḥkām*", reoccurs on an inscription on

the right pier, east door. Yazdani, "Inscriptions of the Khaljī Sultans...", p.24.

48 Inscription on the right pier, west door. Ibid, p.28.

49 Inscription on the left pier, east door. Ibid, p.25.

50 Transcribed and translated by Maulvi Muhammad Ashraf Hussain, *A Record of all the Qur'ānic and non-Historical Epigraphs on the Protected Monuments in the Delhi Province* (Calcutta: Memoirs of the Archaeological Survey of India, no. 47, 1936), p.105.

51 Ibid, pp.109-110.

52 Inscription on the south door, left pier. *"banā farmūd in masjid kī masjid-i jannāt zumreh-yi awliyā wa... ṭabaqah-i atqiyā' wa majma' malā'ik-i kirām wa mahzar-i arwāh-i anbiyā'-yi 'uzzām ast."* I have followed the epigraph as it was transcribed and translated by Page, *Qutub*..., p.37. In this case, Page's reading was less ambitious, but clearer than Yazdani, "Inscriptions of the Khaljī Sultans....", p.27, and plate VIII. For a fuller treatment of 'Alā' al-Dīn and Niẓām al-Dīn's discursive statements see Sunil Kumar, "Assertions of Authority: A Study of the Discursive Statements of Two Sultans of Delhi" in *The Making of Indo-Persian Culture*, ed. Muzaffar Alam, Francoise 'Nalini' Delvoye, Marc Gaborieau (Delhi: Manohar, 2000), pp.37–65.

53 Sijzī, *Fawā'id al-Fu'ād*, pp.18-19: *sakhan dar barkat-i qadam-i nīk mardān uftād: farmūd keh har mauẓā' keh hast, ba-yamn-i aqdām-i ishān murauwah ast, chunāncheh masjid-i jāmi' Dehlī. B'ad az ān farmūd keh, aqdām-i chand awliyā' wa buzurgān ānjah rasīdah bāshad keh ān maqām chunān rāhat dārad.*

54 See Ebba Koch, "The Delhi of the Mughals prior to Shahjahanabad as reflected in the patterns of Imperial visits", in *Art and Culture*, ed. A.J. Qaisar and S.P. Verma (Jaipur: Publication Scheme Press, 1993).

55 In contrast to the very full account of Bābā Farīd, the *Fawā'id al-Fū'ad* provides occasional references to Bakhtiyār Kākī's life and teachings: pp.42-3, 87-8, 104-05, 132, 184-5, 212-3, 246, 268, 315-6, 336, 407, 420. It was in Amīr Khwurd's *Siyār al-Awliyā'*, ed. Sayyid Mandi Ghuri (Lahore: Markaz-i Tahqiqat-i Farsi Iran wa Pakistan, no. 23, Mu'assi-yi Intisharat-i Islami, 1978), pp.48–56, a mid-fourteenth century biographical compendium, that the spiritual genealogy of the Chishtī mystical order was clearly worked out, and Bakhtiyār Kākī's position in the descent of Chishtī saints confirmed.

56 According to Ibn Battuta's evidence, Bakhtiyār Kākī's grave had already become a place of pilgrimage, by the time he visited it in the

mid or late 730s/1330s. Ibn Battuta, *The Travels of Ibn Battuta*, trans. H.A.R. Gibb (Cambridge: University Press, Hakluyt Society, second series, no. 141, 1971), vol. 3, pp.625-6. In 800/1398 the agreement between Mallu Iqbāl Khān and Sultan Nāṣir al-Dīn Maḥmūd Shāh (795–801/1393–99) was reached in the *dargāh* of Bakhtiyār Kākī, see Yaḥyā Sīhrindī, *Ta'rīkh-i Mubārak Shāhī*, ed. M. Hidayat Hosain (Calcutta: Bibliotheca Indica, 1931), p.163. Faced with the threat of Ḥusain Shāh Sharqī's invasion in 883/1478, Bahlul Lôdī prayed at the *dargāh* of the saint. See, Shaikh Rizqullāh Mushtāqī, *Waqī'at-i Mushtāqī*, trans and ed., I.H. Siddiqui (New Delhi: Indian Council of Historical Research, 1993), p.11.

57 *Bābur nāmah*, vol. 2, p.474. Dargāh Qulī Khān, *Muraqqa'-i Dihlī*, ed. and trans. Nurul Hasan Ansari (Delhi: Urdu Department, University of Delhi Press, 1982), pp.23–25, 119–121. The description of Bakhtiyār Kākī's *dargāh* followed accounts of shrines venerating the Prophet's and 'Alī's footprints and it preceded an account of Niẓām al-Dīn Awliyā's tomb.

58 Mughal construction within the *dargāh* is in evidence from the eighteenth century during the reigns of Shāh 'Ālam Bahādur Shāh (1119–24/1707–12), and Farrukh Siyar (1124–31/1713–19). See Sayyid Ahmad Khan, *Āṣār al-Sanādīd*, vol. 1, p.335. The author makes no mention of the floral multi-coloured tiles presumed to have been fixed in the shrine by Aurangzeb, for which, see, Y.D. Sharma, *Delhi and its Neighbourhood*, pp.62-3.

59 Sayyid Ahmad Khan, *Āṣār al-Sanādīd,* vol. 1, p.312.

60 Christian W. Troll, *Sayyid Ahmad Khan: a Reinterpretation of Muslim Theology* (Karachi: Oxford University Press, 1978/79), pp.105, and for his scholarship in the context of the *Āṣār al-Sanādīd* see his "A Note on an Early Topographical work of Saiyid Ahmad Khān: Athār as-Sanādīd", *Journal of the Royal Asiatic Society* (1972): 135–46.

61 Sayyid Ahmad Khān, *Āṣār al-Sanādīd*, vol. 1, p.310–12.

62 It is also one of the reasons why medieval Indian history is so weak in social as well as women's history.

63 This is not to suggest that no historian has questioned the interpretation of the monolithic state and its ruling elite in the medieval period. The writings of scholars such as Muzaffar Alam and Sanjay Subrahmanyam is, however, restricted to the Mughals. For their recent contribution see Muzaffar Alam and Sanjay Subrahmanyam, ed., *The Mughal State,* (Delhi: Oxford University Press, 1998). The writings of Alam, Subrahmanyam and others, however, have not received the circulation

they deserve. Their fate seems to be determined by what Peter Hardy described as "a kind of Gresham's Law" (which continues to operate for the Sultanate period) where "one or two text-books of political history...drive out of intellectual circulation many articles on cultural history in learned periodicals". Peter Hardy, *Historians of Medieval India: Studies in Indo-Muslim Historical Writing* (London: Luzac and Company, 1966 reprint), pp.4-5.

A Medieval Reservoir and Modern Urban Planning
Local Society and the *Ḥauẓ-i Rānī*

In France of the sixteenth century, Lucien Febvre argued, people could not be atheists. In Febvre's reasoning, since the sixteenth century was an age that wanted to "believe", it would be anachronistic to suggest that even as radical a thinker as Rabelais was capable of the sentiment of atheism.[1] If the cultural world of an individual such as Rabelais made it difficult for him to conceive the idea of a world without God, could one argue that in the subcontinent of India in the late twentieth century, most Indians are stuck in the rather paradoxical situation of being familiar with the idea of "secularism", but unsure of its meaning in the practice of their daily lives?

The members of the Constituent Assembly seem to have been aware of the tenuous hold of secular consciousness amongst the larger body of the nation's citizens in 1947 and they had envisaged an important role for the state and government in the popular dissemination of this sentiment. The amended Constitution of India consolidated the sentiment and proclaimed the secular character of the Republic. Article 51A(e) enjoined the nation's citizens "to promote harmony and the spirit of common brotherhood amongst all the people of India transcending religious, linguistic and regional diversities..." What was less clear, however, was the manner in which this spirit of common brotherhood would be introduced and sustained in the nation.

If the people of the nation had to be "taught" and "shepherded" along the secular path, who would teach and guide the government, which was, after all, in the democratic logic of things, constituted of and by the people? The individuals who comprise "the government" are not divorced from the society that they are governing and carry with them many of the thoughts and sensibilities of the people that they are presumably leading into a more humanitarian world. Thus the paradox: if the policies of the Government of India paid regard to the sentiments of social justice and concord present in the constitution, these theories were further processed by social-domestic ideologies resident upon caste, class, or communal sentiments present amongst many government administrators. And since "government" carries legitimate power and authority to introduce and enact policy and change in society, it also occupies the dangerous position of sometimes confirming and disseminating existing prejudices and bigotry as "normal" and authoritative structures in the nation.

I

I thought it would be useful to test my general introductory statements through a study of the history of a medieval reservoir, *ḥauẓ*, located in South Delhi. Although the *Ḥauẓ-i Rānī* was a reservoir that predated the Delhi Sultans (before 1192 CE) it came to be venerated as a sacred area by the local inhabitants in the fourteenth century. As the focus of the city subsequently shifted northwards to Nizamuddin and Shahjahanabad, the sacred character of the *ḥauẓ* became increasingly obscured. It was not until the 1960's and the 1980's when South Delhi started encroaching into the area, that the construction activities of the Delhi Development Authority (DDA) once again focused attention on the *ḥauẓ* which was eventually destroyed. The developments in the 1980's also introduced communal polarisation and tension in the region, not because an erstwhile sacred space had been demolished but because of the nature of the planned development of the region. A "Sports Complex" was constructed on the site, ostensibly as secular a structure as can be. Yet, while the "Sports Complex" might have been planned as a "secular structure", ingrained in its conception were notions of class and confessional distinctions that destroyed older patterns of land usage. The introduction of communal hatred in the region had been far from the intention of the Delhi Development Authority engineers. Yet, in the transposition of their mental universe where the Hindus and Muslims belong to inalienably different moral worlds, it was hardly surprising that the map of the "Sports Complex" sought to construct this social reality in stone and cement. As far as the DDA engineers were concerned, they had constructed a wonderful facility for sport enthusiasts in the city in an "undeveloped" area of the city. They had established order out of chaos; they had abided by the secular principles enshrined in the constitution of the republic, and, without any internal contradiction whatsoever, they had also been honest to their communal prejudices.

II

The *Ḥauẓ-i Rānī*, the "Queen's reservoir", was constructed sometime in the twelfth century, by a queen or a princess, a *Rānī* about whom we possess no further information. In fact, it is only by accident that we can at all glean episodes about the early history of the *Ḥauẓ-i Rānī*. There were other reservoirs in the Delhi plain from the same time period, but most of them have not been remembered. The *Ḥauẓ-i Rānī* was first mentioned in the Persian chronicle of Minhāj-i Sirāj Jūzjānī (completed ca. 1260) only because the city constructed by the early Sultans of Delhi was in its immediate neighbourhood.[2] In the early thirteenth century, the city's major entrance, the Budaun gate was about three hundred metres to the west, and faced the *ḥauẓ*. As a result, people entering the city on one of its major thoroughfares from the *Bāgh-i Jūd* in the north (modern Jorbagh), inevitably passed by its banks. According to Jūzjānī, alongside the *ḥauẓ* was a vast plain which was sometimes used as an army encampment, *lashkargāh*. This area was also used for large ceremonial occasions when, presumably, the space in the city proved deficient.[3] It was near the *ḥauẓ* on the 28th of October, 1242, in the reign of Sultan 'Alā' al-Dīn Mas'ūd (1242–1246), that Sultan Iltutmish's military slaves wrought a terrible punishment upon their political competitors.[4] In 'Alā' al-Dīn Khalajī's reign (1296-1316), it could not have been far from the *Ḥauẓ-i Rānī* that the Sultan set up his major markets. The Sultanate historian, Ẓiyā' al-Dīn Baranī noted that these bazaars were located in the vicinity of the Budaun gate which we know was close to the *ḥauẓ*.[5]

The incidental nature of the information concerning the reservoir notwithstanding, its locale and proximity to the expanding capital of the Delhi Sultans suggests that the *Ḥauẓ-i Rānī* did not occupy a desolate or secluded spot in the Delhi region. In fact, during the Tughluqid period (1320–1414) the area around the *Ḥauẓ-i Rānī* saw considerable building activity. The wall of Muḥammad Shāh Tughluq's (1325-1351) new city of *Jahānpanāh* passed the *ḥauẓ* about two hundred metres to its north. With the construction of *Jahānpanāh* greater efforts were made to regulate the drainage of the seasonal rivulets which meandered their way from their watershed in the Aravalli Hills, towards the River Jumna in the east. One branch of these streams, *nālas*, passed by the west and north wall of the *ḥauẓ*; while another passed some distance away in the east. Since it was necessary to control the flow of these streams as they crossed into the city of *Jahānpanāh*, especially during the monsoon rains, the *Sātpulā* dam was constructed on the city wall, northeast of the *ḥauẓ*.

Through the thirteenth and into the fourteenth century, the area in and around the *Ḥauẓ-i Rānī* underwent substantial transformation. By the early fourteenth century, not merely had this area been the scene of considerable construction activity, but, as the presence of the nearby *Khiṛkī* mosque suggests, it had come to possess a large enough population to warrant the construction of a sizable mosque. The *ḥauẓ* still lay outside the Tughluqid walled city, and suburban access to *Jahānpanāh* was provided by several gates, one of which was named after the *ḥauẓ* the *darwāza'i Ḥauẓ-i Rānī*.[6] We know little about the composition of the population that resided in the vicinity of the *ḥauẓ*; in all likelihood they were service-folk who either worked in the city or provided its markets with produce or artisanal products. Although associated with the material life of the capital, they were distant from its politics and unattached to the household of its elites.

What is significant, however, is that the *ḥauẓ* around which these relatively undistinguished people resided, continued to be repaired well into the Tughluqid period. Its ruined walls today show the presence of the true arch, which in its architectural and stylistic form can only be attributed to the fourteenth-fifteenth centuries. It is doubtful if the local residents themselves possessed the means to carry out this repair work, and in all likelihood it was the Sultan

Photo 1: The west wall of *Ḥauẓ-i Rānī*, a part of the best preserved section. the arches from a later time period (after 1350s) indicate that the *ḥauẓ* continued to draw attention and was periodically improved. (Photographed in 1985)

or his administrative agents who made the necessary investment towards its maintenance.

The construction activity in and around the *ḥauẓ* certainly drew the attention of observers to this local landmark, a regard which also coincided with the ascription of a sacred significance to the reservoir. The hallowed character ascribed to the *ḥauẓ* was unlike the ones attached to reservoirs like *Sūraj Kūnd*, constructed adjacent to a temple for ritual purposes. There is no evidence of the presence of a temple or mosque in the vicinity of the *Ḥauẓ-i Rānī*. In fact, since the name of the *ḥauẓ*—"the Queen's reservoir"— is devoid of any religious significance, it is unlikely that the tank was associated with any deity or sacred occasion. At least to begin with, no special legend, like the one connected with the *Ḥauẓ-i Shamsī* and Sultan Iltutmish's vision of the Prophet Muḥammad, raised the stature of the "Queen's reservoir". Yet the *ḥauẓ* was special because of the unique cultural role that was attached to water in the life of medieval people.

Water, *āb*, was not a plentiful commodity in the central Islamic lands, nor for that matter was it commonly available in the south Delhi plain in the Middle Ages. Its presence was a source of comment, and the Persian terms for cultivation, *ābādānī*, or the terms *ābād* and *ābādī* which meant increasing population and prosperity in a town or district, were derived from the same root, *āb*, or water. The benefactors who made water easily available to the community were singled out for social esteem, and when any great man or woman won social applause because of their altruistic concern for the welfare of the community, it was said that "the drops of rain were entrusted by God in his or her care".[7] In the Middle Ages, water was regarded as the hub of life, of prosperity, a gift given by God. A *ḥauẓ* was special because, amongst its other nourishing qualities, it was an indication that God continued to care by providing capable shepherds for his folk. By the early fourteenth century these sentiments had also started influencing the manner in which local residents regarded the *Ḥauẓ-i Rānī*. Through constant maintenance, not merely was it an exceptionally pleasant place to repair to from the bustle of the town, but it was also a place where one could be close to his Maker. There was some discordance, however, about the identification of the "shepherd" who was associated with the *ḥauẓ*.

By the fourteenth century, many local residents came to believe that it was the famous *Chishtī* mystic saint, Niẓām al-Dīn Awliyā's (died, 1325) association with the *ḥauẓ* which lent significance to the "Queen's reservoir".[8] On the 26th of November, 1315, Nizām al-Dīn narrated the episode of how he came to establish his hospice, *k͟hānaqāh*, in G͟hiyāṣpūr, at that time a small village about five kilometres north of the *ḥauẓ*. The *ṣūfī* saint was fed up with living in the crowded old town of Delhi and was searching for alternative residences without much success. It was while he was at the *Ḥauẓ-i Rānī* and praying for guidance that he received a divine message to go to G͟hiyāṣpūr. The *ṣūfī* saint's reported experiences at the banks of the *ḥauẓ* provided the reservoir with a special venerable status.[9] Proof that the waters of the area possessed a special merit was further provided by Niẓām al-Dīn's spiritual successor Naṣīr al-Dīn Chirāg͟h (d. 1356), who performed his prayer ablutions in the stream adjacent to the *Ḥauẓ-i Rānī*, and read his prayers in the nearby *Sātpul* dam. Together with the veneration that both these Awliyā', "Friends of God", acquired amongst their congregations in Delhi during the fourteenth century, the areas associated with their unique spiritual experiences also gained regard as sacred territories. By the fourteenth century, to many people residing in the vicinity of the *Ḥauẓ-i Rānī*, the reservoir was no longer regarded as just any other *ḥauẓ*; it was the site of a mysterious miracle. And since their habitation was associated with the experiences of a charismatic, holy figure, a "saint" who was close to God and empowered by Him to perform miracles, it also distinguished the residents of the *ḥauẓ* as his special disciples.

The association with the *ṣūfī* saints also served to distance the local residents from the over weaning authority and discourse of the Delhi Sultans. As the "friends of God", the *ṣūfī* saints did not recognize any temporal authority; next to the Prophets themselves, they were the special individuals chosen by God to preserve harmony and stability within the Muslim community. By contrast, the Delhi Sultans claimed that they were the ones who preserved the laws of Islam (*Sharī'a*), the social regulations which allowed individuals the opportunity to live their lives according to the *Qur'ānic* inspiration. Sultan 'Alā' al-Dīn Khalajī's inscriptions on the Delhi congregational mosque stated, for example, that he was the "reviver of the [Muslim] community, the elevator of the banners of the Muslim Holy Law (*Sharī'a*), the strengthener of the foundations and roots of the Muslim religion".[10]

One way the Sultan and his agents could strengthen Islam was by carefully supervising pietistic practices considered to be contrary to the interpretation of the *Sharī'a* as defined by the jurists. *Ṣūfī*s, with their emphasis upon an inner, intuitive understanding of the Holy law and obligations due to their Maker, particularly felt the rigours of this discipline and its stress on appropriate, socially cognisable behaviour.[11] The construction of charitable institutions, schools and mosques were not intended to merely impress subjects of the altruistic and pious conduct of their rulers; these were also places of congregational worship and religious education where Muslims were socialized to accept the jurists's interpretation of the *Sharī'a* and suffer a policing of their conduct to remove "error" in their ritual practise. There was, however, considerable resistance to this coercion, some more dramatic and public than others.[12] But it is important to recognize that the *Ḥauẓ-i Rānī* residents were not rebels; their everyday life was inexorably tied with that of the Sultanate capital. What they sought to preserve, instead, was a degree of autonomy, a space which their *ṣūfī* patron saints created for them.

Another way the Delhi Sultans claimed they were strengthening the "roots of Islam" was by attempting to destroy the foundations of idolatry and all evidence of infidel worship in their territory.

There was the occasional public and dramatic statement of piety when Hindu and Jain temples in the region of Delhi were destroyed, and in the discourse of the court chronicles of the Sultans it was suggested that the righteous wrath of the "protectors of Islam" sought to erase all signs of Hindu habitation from the region of the capital.[13] The presence of the *Ḥauẓ-i Rānī*, however, questioned this "official" representation of the virtuous deeds of the Delhi Sultans. As the name *Ḥauẓ-i Rānī* itself signifies, not merely were old, pre-Sultanate habitations still in existence in the vicinity of Delhi well into the fourteenth century, but the memories of their infidel patron-constructors continued to be perpetuated in their names. Nizām al-Dīn Awliyā', himself, provided the information that *Ḥauẓ-i Rānī* lay within the premises of a garden called the *bāgh-i Jasrath,* the "garden of Jasrath" who was, as his name clarifies, certainly a Hindu.[14] A stone's throw from the court and its vaunted claims concerning the consecration of newly conquered lands through the destruction of the symbols of infidel profanity, resided a community of Muslims who were apparently unconcerned by the past history of their habitat. Indeed, when the local population wanted to articulate their sentiments concerning the sacredness of the *Ḥauẓ-i Rānī*, despite the disfavour of the court towards *ṣūfīs*, they associated the reservoir with the miraculous life of their spiritual master Niẓām al-Dīn Awliyā'. Rather than the *ḥauẓ*'s continued links with a "Hindu past", it was the connection with the Delhi Sultans that was a concern to the area's residents.

The qualities ascribed to the *Ḥauẓ-i Rānī* in the fourteenth century can only be understood in the context of its complicated relationship with the capital of the Delhi Sultanate. On the one hand, the reservoir and its population remained geographically outside the city, and, through a tenuous association with Niẓām al-Dīn Awliyā', lent itself both importance and some autonomy from the influence of the imperial city. On the other hand, the residents in the vicinity of the *ḥauẓ* were sustained by the economic life of the capital. They either worked in the town, or produced goods which were retailed in its markets. Despite all their efforts to the contrary, the prosperity of the *ḥauẓ*, was materially tied to the rhythms of the neighbouring capital. The uneasy association with the powerful agencies resident in the capital, implied a simultaneous attempt on the part of the suburban community to maintain its ties with Delhi, while creating a distance from the court by seeking a distinct, alternate identity.

This close association with the capital also implied that any change in the fortunes of Delhi also had a direct impact upon the *Ḥauẓ-i Rānī* and its neighbours. This was apparent between the sixteenth through the twentieth centuries, when there was a demographic shift in the population settlements in the Delhi plain.[15] The imperial capital had already shifted away from the Delhi region during the reign of Ibrāhīm Lôdī (1517-26) and during the duration of Mughal rule in the sixteenth century, some of its elite population also sought greener pastures away from the old capital. The older Sultanate capitals like *Jahānpanāh* were in palpable decline, and the fifteenth and sixteenth century imperial residences situated in the north of the Delhi plain, *Firūzabād, Dīnpanāh, Salīmgarh*, only manifested occasional flashes of a past glory.[16] The loss of markets and material support for the residents around the *Ḥauẓ-i Rānī* was nothing short of devastating, but equally disastrous was the emergence of the hospice of Niẓām al-Dīn Awliyā' as the primary sacred area associated with the saint's charisma, the major pilgrimage site in the plain of Delhi. With the popularity of the grave shrine, the *ṣūfī* saint's association with the *Ḥauẓ-i Rānī* carried little appreciable significance. The construction of the city of *Shahjahanabad* in the northern segment of the Delhi plain, and the transfer of the Mughal capital in 1648 to that town, further transformed the region around the old ḥ*auẓ* into an outback.

Even when the last of the Mughal emperors, and some notables from the city of *Shahjahanabad*, started establishing residences in south Delhi in the early nineteenth century, their hunting lodges or summer homes were located mainly to the west of *Ḥauẓ-i Rānī*, in the Mehrauli area near the Qutb. *Ḥauẓ-i Rānī* remained unaffected by the change in the fortunes of Mehrauli and while it continued to figure as a "reservoir" on nineteenth century British land survey maps of the Delhi plain, the Gazetteer of the Delhi district admitted that by 1883-4 the *ḥauẓ* was no more than a seasonal swamp with its lands occupied by a mango grove.[17]

The gradual silting and ruin of the *ḥauẓ* by the nineteenth century does not mean that the area of the reservoir lost all significance to the local Muslim residents. A village called Hauz Rani was established near the reservoir, on the ruined walls of the *Jahānpanāh* fort. Sometime in the nineteenth century the banks of the "Queen's reservoir" started being used by the villagers as a graveyard. The choice of the area as a graveyard might have been motivated by considerations of convenient accessibility to the village, and, perhaps, by the presence of a grove of trees, incongruous in the midst of the flat, monotonous farmland, reminiscent of the garden of paradise. It is doubtful if in the nineteenth century, the memory of the *ḥauẓ*'s special significance derived from the *ṣūfī* saints was at all alive. Instead in the history that was ascribed to the area at this time, the tank was no longer a sacred place imbued by the *barakat* or the grace of the mystic saints; it was merely a graveyard where some of the esteemed members of the village were buried. Together with the other changes which had occurred in the old city of Delhi by the nineteenth century, the *ḥauẓ* of the *Ḥauẓ-i Rānī* had also become unimportant in the popular imagination of its residents.

III

When I first wandered through this area in 1975, the city had again started intruding into the region of the *Ḥauẓ-i Rānī*. The first houses in the neighbouring suburb of Saket had started to be built and the Delhi Development Authority (DDA) had already notified and appropriated most of the fields belonging to the residents of Shaikh Sarai and Hauz Rani villages. In the transfer of land ownership little attention had been paid to the *ḥauẓ*, and, in the process of notification, the DDA had taken over half of the reservoir. The remaining half was left with the villagers as their graveyard and common property. In the master plan for Saket, the area of the *ḥauẓ* in the possession of the DDA was earmarked for a sports complex. But even before the construction work could start, the Delhi Development Authority dug a *pucca nāla*, a storm water drain through the southern wall of the *ḥauẓ*, trapping and diverting the old rivulet away from the *Jahānpanāh* city wall.

The response of the Hauz Rani villagers to the intrusion of the Delhi Development Authority was by and large supportive. Some of the larger landlords did complain about the compensation paid to them for the lands notified by the government, but the majority saw in the recent developments signs of "progress". While most of the residents of the village were aware of the presence of an old reservoir near their graveyard, they could only talk positively of the *pucca nāla* that had destroyed a part of the *Ḥauẓ-i Rānī*. Because of the new drainage system, the old silted streams no longer flooded the village every other monsoon.

The 1970's and 1980's were dynamic years of transformation for the village of Hauz Rani. As construction in the suburb of Saket and adjoining Pushp Vihar gathered speed, Hauz Rani emerged as their satellite, providing commercial services to the building industry. Many of the older residents of the village were the plumbers, electricians, welders, carpenters, masons and daily wage labourers to their new neighbours. There was some transfer of property as Hindus and Jains set up their supply and repair stores at the fringes of the village facing Saket. Together with the change in a life-style dependent upon a salaried or contractual relationship with an employer resident outside the social world of the village, the intrusion of the rhythms and comportment of a city life-style, marked the difficult period as the village made the transition into a suburb of New Delhi.

Greater earnings went hand in hand with lower self esteem as Hauz Rani residents recognized their status within a social hierarchy where the professional and business classes of the neighbouring residential areas were far and away the more privileged group. The economic disparity was further accentuated by the confessional divide which characterized the distinctions between the suburbs. The majority of the people living in Saket, Malaviya Nagar and Pushp Vihar were Hindu, followed by Sikh, Jain and finally, a miniscule Christian and Muslim population. In Hauz Rani, only the newer residents on the peripheries of the village were Hindu, Sikh or Jain; the core remained Muslim. The "inner-outer" geographical distribution of communities within Hauz Rani mirrored the manner in which the Muslim residents of the village sought to deal with the outside world. In their relationships with an "outside" world, Hauz Rani Muslims presented a non-denominational, almost "professional" face. It was only as you entered the "inner regions" of the village that the significance of the mosque, the *maulvī* preacher, the pictures of the *Ka'ba* in cigarette and barber saloons, the pavement *kabab* vendors with their meat delicacies, and the butchers selling buffalo meat, manifested the presence of an alternate world.

One should not, however, make too much of a case for the class and confessional divide between the neighbouring suburbs at this time, or the fact that the Hauz Rani village possessed an "inner" face, an alternate world. Although largely Muslim, the confessional bond did not create the sense of a united community amongst the residents of the village. Despite sharing a common cultural and religious heritage, the social relationships within the village, and with members outside, were also influenced by a wide range of material considerations. Nor was the Hauz Rani village, in the 1970's and 1980's, a closed or defensive realm; there were significant breaches which muted the divisions between the village and the adjoining neighbourhood of Saket. Important in this context were the parched lands of what had once been a part of the old *Ḥauẓ-i Rānī* reservoir.

Although the DDA had constructed a "sports complex" on their portion of the *ḥauẓ*, at this stage of development it constituted three large fields without any barriers distinguishing the open spaces, the *maidāns*, from the village burial, and common grounds. Saket residents and the Hauz Rani villagers moved freely throughout the area. In fact, in a fit of rare sensitivity, the DDA constructed a paved pedestrian path and bridge that passed through a grove of trees near the village common ground and connected Saket with Hauz Rani. The absence of barriers between the two neighbourhoods was apparent in that children from Saket played football every evening, ten to fifteen a side, with their peers from Hauz Rani. The very absence of a structured sports regimen allowed for an unregulated fraternizing between the residents of the two neighbourhoods. The people of Saket were unaware of the presence of a *ḥauẓ* in their vicinity and only some of the older Hauz Rani villagers reflected about the history of their graveyard. As far as one could make out, the lands of the old *Ḥauẓ-i Rānī* had lost their history and effectively become desacralized. It had also become one of those rare areas where, at least for some time, people forgot their class, ethnic and confessional differences.

The DDA was directly responsible for demarcating and developing this secular lung in an area witnessing the introduction of class and sectarian distinctions. But this was only by accident; their actual intentions for the *Ḥauẓ-i Rānī* area were clarified in 1990 when the interim sports complex was razed and supplanted by its more elaborate version.

In the place of the accessible, open *maidāns* left free for unstructured activities, the new Saket Sports Complex was open only to members for squash, badminton, tennis, table-tennis, cricket, jogging, basketball, aerobics, yoga and horse-riding. The Hauz Rani villager's competence hardly extended into these exalted realms, and by default, if nothing else, the new Sports Complex was not visualized to cater to the poorer segment of the city's population. When I queried the DDA engineers about their plans for the development of this area, they were very forthright in establishing the connection between the Sports Complex and the neighbourhood

Photo 2: The east wall of the *ḥauẓ* with a part of the village graveyard in the background. in the groves of tress. The pedestrian path connecting the village of Hauz Rani and Saket skirted the graveyard. The openness of the area, photographed in 1985, stands in contrast to photographs 3 and 5.

of Saket, with its upper middle-class residential profile. Even if it had been constructed on [only half of] the bed of the old *ḥauẓ*, the orientation of the Sports Complex was certainly not towards the Hauz Rani village.

The class bias which was evident in the construction of the new Sports Complex was however only incidental to its overall conceptualization. The real problem for the DDA was posed by the fact that it was in the vicinity of a "low-class" Muslim village and its graveyard. Here "class" was understood in more than its economic implications and encompassed the host of Muslim practises that the Hindu engineers of the Delhi Development Authority found abhorrent. Not the least of these was the practice of burial, or more prosaically, the practice of indiscriminate interring of corpses. As it was rather colourfully explained to me, not merely was burial unhygienic because it attracted maggots and other sundry vermin, but since these were largely unbuilt graves covered with earth, people were forever stumbling onto them. It was a filthy unhygienic practice, and as a guard at the Sports Complex explained to me, "No matter how deep you buried a corpse, its odour nevertheless permeated the region". People who observed this ritual were not merely unclean, but they did not accept the norms of society as the Hindus or the DDA engineers understood them. Amongst the other cultural values ascribed to the Muslim residents of Hauz Rani by the planners of the Sports Complex (and I presume that these were believed to be more general qualities shared by the entire community) were hysteria, unruliness, pilfering, and a communal sentiment which made fraternizing impossible.

Thus, if the Saket Sports Complex was to be a successful DDA

Photo 3: The only entrance to the village graveyard and the *ḥauẓ*. Note the sign proclaiming the "old graveyard". Photographed in 1991

project, its development had to include plans whereby it could be insulated from the hostile environment posed by the Muslim village. The remedy lay in zoning the areas where the villagers were permitted entry. This was now restricted by stone and barbed wire walls to include only the approach to the half of the *ḥauẓ* which fell within the common property and graveyard of the village.

The Sports Complex itself was enclosed by towering walls and reoriented towards a solitary entrance approached from Saket. The pedestrian pathway connecting the two neighbourhoods was also fenced in and secured by two gates which were patrolled at night.

If the DDA sought to divide and insulate the two communities, the reactions of the villagers only accentuated the distance and mistrust which pervaded the area of the *Ḥauẓ-i Rānī*. Despite the fact

Photo 4: The Sports Complex boundary walls divide the once green spaces. Photographed in 1991

that the area of the Sports Complex had been land legally notified by the DDA, the sudden and obtrusive denial of access to land and freedom, was ascribed a more nefarious and long term design. The villagers were convinced that the government intended to eventually expel them from their common property and graveyard as well. They became acutely aware of their minority community status and sought to defend their lands. This implied a systematic destruction of the half of the *ḥauẓ* which fell into the share of the Hauz Rani village. Its walls were pillaged to build goat and buffalo pens, and all paths into the area were barricaded with thorn and bristle bushes.

Photo 5: The east wall of the *ḥauẓ* photographed in 1991 from about the same spot as the one taken in 1985 (Photo 3). The villagers have started using the old *ḥauẓ* walls for their cattle.

The villagers sought further protection by constructing a sacred history linking the lands of Hauz Rani with their ancestors. Ironically it was not the history of the *Ḥauẓ-i Rānī* that the villagers chose to embellish, but that of the graveyard, now regarded as a sacred place

Photo 6: The interior of a buffalo pen built into the side of the esat wall of *ḥauẓ*.

where the ancient progenitors of the current villagers, all *Sayyids* (descendents of the Prophet Muḥammad), were buried. Placards

Photo 7: The villagers, ironically, pointed to unattended graves such as this as evidence of their long presence in the neighbourhood. Most of these graves are, however, not that old and in considerable disrepair.

were placed around the graveyard emphasizing its historicity as an ancient burial ground, *qadīm qabristān*. With one stroke not merely had the villagers claimed rights to these lands from antiquity, but, as descendants of *Sayyids*, they were by extension related to the Prophet. Only the ignorant could call them "low class" now.

The response of the Hauz Rani villagers to the DDA challenge, also provoked a public articulation of their Muslim identity. Mosques were renovated and repainted and children enrolled in schools of religious instruction. In a disarming conversation between a preacher and a small congregation that I eavesdropped upon in a mosque, I managed to savour the "facts" of Indian history taught to the children of the area. The *imām* explained to his audience, that there had occasionally been governments, *ḥukūmat*, in the past that had denigrated Islam and heaped injustice upon God's chosen community. There was, for example, the apostate

Mughal emperor Akbar (1556-1605), and in modern times there was the current Hindu government, but God would give to each of them His chosen retribution at the Day of Judgment. Clearly the heroes of the Hauz Rani villagers were no longer those of the Indian republic.

Across the great divide, the response of the Saket residents to the Sports Complex differed completely from the villagers. There was immediate support to the building activity introduced in their vicinity by the DDA. On the one hand, the proximity of such an elite facility to Saket was appreciated for its positive impact in improving the profile of the neighbourhood amongst the New Delhi suburbs. It was assumed that rental rates in Saket could now be legitimately inflated. On the other hand, Saket property owners were also pleased by the security precautions. They had not quite forgotten the trauma of the 1984 riots after Mrs. Gandhi's assassination, when (what was assumed to be) lumpen mobs had looted Sikh business and domestic establishments. At that time, neighbourhood vigilante groups had patrolled the streets against a faceless enemy, but they had been sure that the adversary was poor and desperate, and that not just Sikh but all middle-class homes were legitimate targets. By 1990, many of the Saket householders had provided an address, if not a face to the enemy; they knew that their adversaries resided in Hauz Rani. After a burglary in "M" block Saket, so sure had the victims been of the provenance of the thieves, that in their rage they had sought to sever links with the village by demolishing the bridge leading to the pedestrian path connecting the two neighbourhoods. Their worst suspicions were confirmed when the DDA also identified the Muslim villagers as a threat, and they applauded the security measures which distanced the two realms. The harmonious fraternization that had occurred between neighbourhoods in the *maidāns* of the *Ḥauẓ-i Rānī* just a few years ago, suddenly seemed a lifetime away.

IV

The Saket Sports Complex was conceived and designed as a recreational facility which would encourage physical fitness and competitive sports, all positive sentiments. Within its limited context, it was a wonderful complex which, it could be argued, successfully accomplished its goals. Nor had the engineers of the Delhi Development Authority intended to introduce a communal polarization between the Saket and Hauz Rani neighbourhoods. In fact, the Saket Sports Complex was a very "secular" institution, and its definitions of "secularism" originated from the constitution of India no less. Its brochure clarified that as a facility constructed by the government for the public, the Saket Sports Complex sought to "induce...[a] ...spirit of mutual help and goodwill among citizens of Delhi" and membership was open to all individuals without respect to caste or creed. The only qualification was a prior sports record and the ability to pay the membership fees. Nevertheless, as we have noticed, these declarations of secular principles hardly served to promote goodwill within the *Ḥauẓ-i Rānī* region.

It needs to be remembered, however, that there was a phase of "development" when in fact the DDA had successfully bridged gaps between class and sectarian differences which had started to manifest themselves in this area. The open fields of the interim sports complex provided the liminal space which eased the differences between communities, presenting an opportunity to strangers to establish acquaintances outside their familiar social realms. The free access and unstructured nature of the leisure activities placed no premium on class or confessional differences. For the moment people were accepted as individuals and not as extensions of their separate social worlds. On the contrary, the process of fraternization provided the opportunity for doubting the validity of the many inherited clichéd sentiments about unfamiliar people. Not merely was this sports complex secular and democratic, but it could also have proved to be an agent for neutralizing a potential class and communal polarization between neighbourhoods.

The problem, of course, lay in the fact that this sports complex was still perceived to be "undeveloped". It was unable to maximize its potential since it lacked the structure of a formal sports arena. If the "openness" of the original complex was its weakness, the prescribed "limits" and "discipline" of the new one were its strengths. The new Sports Complex promised limited membership, discipline in dress and conduct of members, coaching, and facilities where the rules of the game would be followed. This was an exclusive world available only to the familiar. The old cohabitants were suddenly relegated by the DDA to the other side of the boundary as foreigners and threats. The liminality of the *maidāns* was lost and the newly resplendent Sports Complex presented an unmistakable class, and confessional bias, strikingly apparent to those suddenly ostracised from the area.

I had suggested in the introductory comments to this paper that despite the awareness of secularism as a positive, just and progressive ideology, most Indians were unsure of its substantive meaning in the context of everyday practice. In the light of the *Ḥauẓ-i Rānī* episode that I have just described I would further clarify that a large number of Indians are secular from time to time in their everyday lives without being aware of the significance of their practice. As had happened in the sports complex of yore, and still occurs in some places, people of differing backgrounds–caste, class, region–continue to meet equably in diverse situations, and strike common, individuatistic, human equations. These transpire frequently enough in the proscribed course of one's daily life and certain situations and places – educational institutions, travel, pilgrimage – increase the opportunities for this kind of intermingling. Yet, in the definition of human activities, these everyday happenings are not signified for their potential importance in creating a secular mentality and little effort is made to preserve or encourage them. Such occasions were more readily available in the past, but they were not valued and, as in the case of the *Ḥauẓ-i Rānī* the open social spaces are being encroached. Thus the opportunities available to individuals to momentarily relinquish their more particular forms of social identification, permit a dialogue with dissimilar people and allow for the growth of a secular sentiment are diminishing.

It is not my argument that the existence of these arenas of informal social mingling will in themselves allow for the presence of a secular sentiment in our society. Secularism needs the protection of constitutional guarantees, but its everyday practice also needs to be cherished and defended. Without it secularism only carries a notional definition.

The ritual genuflection to secular sentiments was certainly present in the brochure of the Saket Sports Complex, and its construction had received the patronage of the Congress-I and the Janata Dal, all self-proclaimed secular political parties. This secularism had meant precious little to the DDA engineers, whose class and community biases distanced the neighbouring Muslim villagers from the *Ḥauẓ-i Rānī*. As a final mockery of the secular spirit, the DDA chose to approach a Muslim, the Janata Dal Home Minister, Mufti Mohammad Sayeed, to inaugurate the Sports Complex and legitimise all their actions. The villagers perception of the developments in the *ḥauẓ* were perhaps justified. They looked beyond the secular platitudes of the DDA Sports Complex brochure, and the Muslim chief guest; in reflecting upon the changes in their own lives they saw instead, a triumph of the Hindu *ḥukūmat*.

Notes

1 Lucien Febvre, *The Problem of Unbelief in the Sixteenth Century: The Religion of Rabelais*, trans. B. Gottlieb (Cambridge: Harvard University Press, 1982). Febvre's generalisations have been questioned most notably by Carlo Ginzberg, *The Cheese and the Worms: the Cosmos of a Sixteenth century Miller*, trans. John and Anne Tedeschi (New York: Penguin Books, 1982 reprint), pp. xxiii-xxiv, 133-4. Although Febvre's provocative generalisations are problematical, they serve a useful purpose in guarding us against anachronistic

characterisations of material and belief structures (in the plural) maintained and ascribed by different social groups in the historical past.

2 Minhāj-i Sirāj Jūzjānī, *Ṭabaqāt-i Nāṣirī*, vol. 1, p. 469.

3 *Ibid*, vol. 2, pp. 81-2.

4 *Ibid*, vol. 1, p. 469, vol. 2, p. 27.

5 Ẓiyā' al-Dīn Baranī, *Ta'rīkh-i Firūz Shāhī*, p. 309.

6 S.H. Hodivala, *Studies in Indo-Muslim History* (Bombay: Popular Book Depot, 1957), vol. 2, p. 144.

7 Fakhr-i Mudabbir, *Ādāb al-Mulūk wa kifāyat al-Mamlūk*, ed. Muhammad Sarwar Maulavi (Teheran, Haidari, 1976), p.16. See also H. Ringgren, "Some Religious Aspects of the Caliphate", in *The Sacral Kingship*, (Leiden: E.J. Brill, 1959), pp. 737-47.

8 Unlike Christianity and its institutionalised forms of canonisation of saints, the recognition of a saint (*walī*, "friend of God") in Islam was the result of a social consensus concerning the exceptionally pietistic qualities of an individual. Several participants were involved in the creation of this "social consensus", not least of all the aspirant himself, but it also included disciples who embellished and popularised the qualities of their master. Niẓām al-Dīn, in particular, was extremely fortunate to have amongst his disciples, litteratures of the calibre of Amīr Ḥasan Sijzī, Amīr Khusrau and Ẓiyā' al-Dīn Baranī, whose writings spread the virtues of their teacher to a huge audience beyond the limits of his immediate congregation in Delhi. On the question of "sainthood" in Islam, see P.M Currie, *The Shrine and Cult of Mu'īn al-Dīn Chishtī of Ajmer* (Delhi: Oxford University Press, 1989), and on the "process" of disseminating the charisma of a saint see Richard Eaton, "The Political and Religious authority of the Shrine of Baba Farid: in *Moral Conduct and Authority*, ed., Barbara Metcalf (Berkeley: University of California Press,1984), Bruce B. Lawrence, "The Earliest Chishtiya and Shaikh Nizam ud-din Awliya", in *Delhi Through the Ages: Essays in Urban History, Culture and Society*, ed. R. E. Frykenberg (Delhi: Oxford University Press, 1986) and Sunil Kumar, "Assertions of Authority: a Study of the Discursive Statements of Two Sultans of Delhi", and chapter 5 in this book.

9 Amīr Ḥasan Sijzī, *Fawā'id al-Fu'ād*, p. 242; Amīr Khwurd, *Siyar al-Awliyā'*, p.120.

10 G. Yazdani, "Inscriptions of the Khalji Sultans of Delhi and their contemporaries in Bengal", *Epigraphia Indo-Moslemica* (1917-18), pp. 8-42.

11 Sunil Kumar, "Assertions of Authority", pp. 37-65.

12 See Sunil Kumar, "Qutb and Modern Memory" in this volume.

13 *Ibid.*

14 Sijzī, *Fawā'id al-Fu'ād,* p. 242. In Hindu myth, Jasrath/Dasrath was an ancient king of Ayodhya, better known as the father of Rama, the celebrated hero of the epic *Ramayana*. The *bāgh-i Jasrath* was probably an orchard, or a grove of trees rather than the formal Mughal *chahār bāgh* the walled-in garden, or the Victorian gardens popular in India today.

15 See also Sunil Kumar, "Making Sacred History or everyone his/her own Historian: the Pasts of the village of Saidlajab" in this volume.

16 Ebba Koch, "The Delhi of the Mughals prior to Shahjahanabad as reflected in the patterns of Imperial Visits".

17 Anonymous, *A Gazetter of Delhi* (Gurgaon: Vintage Books, 1988 reprint). See also H. C. Fanshawe, *Delhi Past and Present* (Gurgaon: Vintage Books, 1991 reprint), Map 8.

Making Sacred History or Everyone his/her own Historian

The Pasts of the Village of Saidlajab[1]

I

All of us, whether we realise it or not, function as historians. In our own different ways we constantly process information about our past – concerning our family, the work place, our community, even the nation – and seek the aid of a multitude of sources to joggle our memories – letters, diaries, written messages, oral testimonies, photographs, or the media. Few of us would claim, however, that the exercise of processing information about our past was carried out with the arcane interests of most (boring) professional historians. We are most frequently interested in only our own immediate past, to provide some context to our present and to perhaps enable us to make "wiser" decisions about our future. Yet we ascribe fairly long histories to other parts of our reasoning. Most of us would find it extremely disconcerting to accept that our religious faith, or things which we regard as sacred and holy, had only an immediate history. Even if we do not remember the unfortunate history classes of our youth and cannot date our scriptures and beliefs with any certainty, we are confident that they originated in early antiquity and this hardly needs any substantiation; proof is readily available in almost everything that we read, hear and watch daily.

Sacred beliefs are quite naturally holy cows and many of us prefer not to question or tamper with them. But this is where we tend to mortgage the historian within all of us. We accept in our daily lives that the experience of yesterday will help us cope with the present and the future, tacitly recognising that life is a dynamic process and that no two days will be quite alike. We constantly remind ourselves of our past mistakes so that we may avoid them in the future and we store information to ensure that our memory does not fail us on this score. Despite our successes and frustrations we recognise the presence of historical change in our society which we try in our own frail ways to understand and deal with. But this understanding of change does not extend into the realm of the sacred; since it is not the realm of mortals suddenly the laws of history no longer apply.

It was in this context that I thought I would explore how some elements from the past came to possess historical significance. I have studied this through the history of Saidlajab, a village in south Delhi where a shrine was ascribed with sacred qualities in the middle ages. Over the passage of time the sacred element of this shrine was lost and replaced by other points of significance which had nothing to do with its original formulation. In what came to be the eventual history of the village, structures which were actually constructed at a much later time than the original shrine were subsequently attributed with religious significance. Nor has the making and remaking of the sacred history of this monument occured in a historical vacuum. It is interesting to note that the reassignation of religious domain took place in the context of an existing conflict over territory between opposing groups of people. And, not surprisingly, mortals had a big hand in defining what was eventually sacred in Saidlajab.

II

Saidlajab is a small village located to the east of the Qutb minar, just south of the New Delhi suburb of Saket. Today the village is inhabited almost entirely by Jats and Mewatis, although increasingly a migrant population is setting up a flourishing commercial and industrial base on its fringes. Its proximity to Saket has driven up property and rental rates and the village is inundated by all the evidence of city consumerism. To a traveller on the Mehrauli-Badarpur road the fleeting glimpse of Saidlajab provides a picture not unlike many truck-stops: dhabas, mechanic shops, and an aggressive, self-confident population.

Saidlajab however, is an old village, and the name is a corruption of *Sayyid al-Ḥujjāb*, a notable of the fourteenth century who resided in the area where the current village is located. The Sayyid who was also known as Ma'rūf, or the famous one, was a chamberlain, *ḥājib*, in the court of the Sultan Firūz Shāh Tug̲h̲luq (1351-1388). He was also a descendent of the Prophet, had performed the *ḥajj* and his title *Sayyid al-Ḥujjāb* reflected the distinction that he had won for himself: the head of all the court chamberlains. The chronicler Shams Sirāj 'Afīf included a short biography of the Sayyid in his *Ta'rīk̲h̲-i Firūz Shāhī*, where he mentioned that Ma'rūf was a name given to the Sayyid by the *ṣūfī* Niẓām al-Dīn Awliyā' who had prescient knowledge of the boy's future greatness.[2] Ma'ruf was an extremely devout person widely respected for his piety and concern to follow the *sharī'a* in his daily life. He had served Sultan Muḥammad Shāh Tug̲h̲luq (1325-1351) but was a particularly close confidant, *nadīm*, to Firūz Shāh Tug̲h̲luq. According to Shams Sirāj 'Afīf the Sayyid had sufficient influence with the Sultan to calm his temper and revoke such orders that were given in haste or anger.[3]

While he was in the service of Firūz Shāh Tug̲h̲luq, Ma'ruf must have resided near his Sultan in Firūzabād, but he also had a residence just south of Jahānpanah outside the south-eastern wall of the first city of Delhi called Dihlī-i Kuhnā, or "Old Delhi". This was probably constructed while he had been in the service of

Muḥammad Shāh Tug͟hluq and the court was located in Jahānpanah. In Firūz Tug͟hluq's reign this residence must have been seldom used; the Sultan could not bear to have him away for any length of time. It was, therefore, only after his master's death that Ma'rūf returned permanently to south Delhi.

In his years of service as *ḥājib* with the Delhi Sultan, Ma'rūf had won public acclaim as one who interceded with the Sultan on behalf of the indigent and the afflicted. To some extent this was hardly surprising; the Sayyid's piety and high moral qualities had already been foretold by none other than the mystic saint Niẓām al-Dīn Awliyā'. Thus, Ma'rūf's altruism was in keeping with his saintly personality which had also won him the regard of the Sultan. After the Sayyid's death these saintly qualities were obviously not forgotten, and as the graves in the vicinity of his residence in south Delhi suggest, his followers expected their master to intercede on their behalf in the court of the High Majesty on the Day of Judgement. The *barakat* or the grace of the holy person imbued the sacred area where he was buried and protected those who chose to reside there.

III

It is not clear exactly how long after Ma'rūf's death, the reputation of his holiness continued to attract disciples to his hospice. It is doubtful for instance, if people in the sixteenth century held Ma'rūf in as high a regard as before, and he is not included amongst the many pious remembered in the *Siyar al-'Ārifīn* or the *Ak͟hbār al-Ak͟hyār*, biographical encyclopaedias of mystics completed in the sixteenth century.[4] Nor does Abū'l Faẓl mention him in the *Ā'īn-i Akbarī* amongst the pious men, once resident in Delhi.[5] By the standards of veneration paid to saints over long periods of time, *Sayyid al-Ḥujjāb* seems to have had a relatively brief innings. Yet, the Sayyid's diminished popularity should not be attributed to "deficiencies" in his spiritual merit; instead the composition of the residents in the village underwent continuous change from the fifteenth centuriy onwards and in displacing the old inhabitants, the new migrants also altered the original *raison d'etre* of the settlement.

The original residents of *Sayyid al-Ḥujjāb* in the fourteenth century had been the dependents of Ma'rūf who continued to reside near the grave of their master. It was a small settlement whose inhabitants worked the fields in the neighbourhood and relied upon the Tughluqid government to provide an umbrella of security from the neighbouring Mewatis. As the late Sultanate chronicles, the *Ta'rīkh-i Mubārak Shāhī* and the *Ta'rīkh-i Muḥammadī* describe however, Firūz Shāh Tughluq's successors lacked the military capacity of their predecessors to intervene effectively in the southern suburbs of their own capital.[6] Timūr's plunder of Delhi (1398-99) robbed the Sultanate of the little prestige it had commanded, and other than the provinces of the empire, even the suburbs of Delhi challenged the Delhi Sultan's commands.[7]

From the late fourteenth century onward a migration of Mewatis, and Jats occured in the southern peripheries of the Delhi plain. Of the two groups the Mewatis were the more predominant and for short periods had political control of the southern suburbs. Towards the end of the fourteenth century, Bahādur Nahīr Mewatī negotiated with the Tughluqid Sultans Nāṣir al-Dīn Muḥammad Shāh (1390-93), Nāṣir al-Dīn Maḥmūd Shāh Tughluq (1393-1395, 1399-1413) and Nuṣrat Shāh (1395-99) from Mehrauli and Dihlī-i Kuhnā,[8] and for some time during 'Alā' al-Dīn 'Ālam Shāh Sayyid's reign (1446-1451) Aḥmad Khān Mewati ruled from Lādū Sarāy, a village about a thousand metres from the old village of *Sayyid al-Ḥujjāb*.[9] The Mewatis who migrated into these regions were Muslims and in *Sayyid al-Ḥujjāb* they either expelled the older inhabitants or seized their more productive lands. In their bid to place their own authoritative stamp upon the village they disregarded the faith of the older inhabitants in the shrine of *Sayyid al-Ḥujjāb* and constructed their own mosques in the village. In effect, while the settlement continued to bear the Sayyid's name, the significance of *Sayyid al-Ḥujjāb* in the lives of the peasants inhabiting the village started becoming insignificant.

The process of Mewati and Jat immigration into the village of *Sayyid al-Ḥujjāb* must have continued through the period of Mughal rule but as the information in the *Ā'īn-i Akbarī* suggests, there was a noticeably larger movement of Jats from the late sixteenth century onwards. According to Abū'l Faẓl, by this time period, the population of Palam was largely Jat in composition and in the general area of the old suburban districts of Delhi, Jats and Chauhan Rajputs predominated.[10] The Jat element in the rural population of these areas must have increased and derived greater confidence from the late seventeenth and early eighteenth century peasant rebellions in western U.P., and under Chaurāman Jat they successfully tested the might of the Mughal empire. By the end of their rebellions as one observer noted "all the parganas under Agra and Delhi had been sacked and plundered and, from the tumult of [the] perdition seeker [Chaurāman Jat], the routes and ways were blocked".[11] It is doubtful if the village of *Sayyid al-Ḥujjāb* was directly affected by these uprisings, but the predominantly (Hindu)-Jat composition of the village probably dates from this period. As Sir Henry M. Elliot's information brings out, the overweaning presence of Jats amongst the village residents of the *Sayyid al-Ḥujjāb* area was in clear evidence by 1844.[12]

The social consequences of this demographic change are not clear, but with the change in the balance between the Hindu-Jat and Muslim-Mewati residents, wider alterations in land proprietorships must have occured. These land transactions had certainly been accomplished by the beginning of the twentieth century. In 1913 when Zafar Hasan carried out his *Survey of Mohammadan and Hindu monuments in Delhi* he had noticed that the *khānaqāh* (hospice) of *Sayyid al-Ḥujjāb* was owned by

Khem Chand and housed his family, a mosque in the village was jointly owned by Tulsi, Nathu, Nanak and Cheku who resided on the premises, and a tomb was owned and converted into a dwelling by one Ratia.[13] Zafar Hasan had also noticed that the village contained a mosque with a sizeable courtyard whose income had been set aside sometime in the past as a *waqf* for charitable purposes.[14] The relative unimportance of the Muslim population in this village at the turn of the century was evident, however, in the fact that this *waqf* land remained barren and unused.

IV

By the 1940's the changes in the *Sayyid al-Ḥujjāb* village were even more dramatic. The communal tensions of the decade and the increasing minority status of the Muslims in the village had led them to seek security through migration into the nearby villages of Shaikh Sarai or farther away in Nizamuddin and Shahjahanabad. As a result in the 1980's *Sayyid al-Ḥujjāb* did not possess a single Muslim family. The total marginalisation of the Muslim population and the complete loss of the original significance and character of the village is perhaps best brought out by the changes which occured in its name. In a topographical map of Delhi drawn in 1807 by the British, *Sayyid al-Ḥujjāb* was corrupted into Sieud Lujab. While we are aware that spelling was not one of the strong points of the British – the map spells Safdar Jung as Sufter Jung, Mehrauli as Moorali – yet these misspellings did not pass into history; many were subsequently corrected.[15] In the case of *Sayyid al-Ḥujjāb*, however, since the name of the village meant nothing to its inhabitants it continued to evolve imaginatively until Sieud Lujab was contracted to become the present Saidlajab. This was also convenient: when the present residents of the village narrated their history to me they were convinced that they were the original inhabitants of Saidlajab, their ancestors had resided and cultivated the neighbouring fields since the dawn of time. At least as far as they were concerned *Sayyid al-Ḥujjāb* had never existed.

Photo 1: The mosque in the *waqf* area. Photographed in 1985.

As historians can get to be, the villagers were altogether a little bit too glib in narrating their history. As it turned out they were not entirely unaware that the history of their village included other earlier residents who were, for one or the other reason, no longer with them. When I first visited Saidlajab in 1985 I was chasing ruins which I thought might exist in a village which figured in old land survey maps of Delhi. Most villagers were unaware about any ruins, but one directed me to the village dump. This was a fairly large area, overgrown with thorny shrubs and thickets, used by the village women to make their dung cakes, and its entrance was filled with garbage and refuse. In the centre of this area was a partially ruined mosque, and at some distance a few graves. Whereas the rest of the village was marked by dense construction, this large expanse of land was strangely free of all buildings. I later realised that this was the *waqf* property that Zafar Hasan had described in his survey.

On the day I visited this area some Muslims were also present and they introduced themselves as visitors from Meerut. These gentlemen were in the process of cleaning up the garbage and refuse

Photo 2: The grave identified as that of 'Sayyid sahib'. Note the green *chādar*, the north-south orientation of the grave and the attempts to clean the neighbouring area.

from the mosque and its environs. The process of cleansing also centred around a grave near the mosque over which a green silk veil,

Photo 3: The southern area of the *waqf* land. Note the refuge and unkempt area beyond the grave. Photographed in 1985.

chādar, had been placed, incense sticks lit, and the surrounding area sprinkled with rose water; cleansing and sacralisation of the grave were obviously linked agendas. The grave had been identified as belonging to Sayyid-sahib and since at that time I was ignorant of *Sayyid al-Ḥujjāb* my hosts were kind enough to narrate the saint's great moral qualities and miracles which proved that he was one of the *Awliyā'*, friends of God.

The attempt to sacralise their *pīr*'s tomb symbolised the winning back of the *waqf* territory which was used and occupied by the villagers as their de facto common ground. The line demarcating the cleansed area and the village area filled with dung cakes was as significant as any political frontier. The Muslims from Meerut had ambitions of getting electricity and water connections, of repairing the mosque and starting the prayer and '*urs*, the death anniversary celebrations for the Sayyid.

I next went back to Saidlajab in 1986 to discover the victors in the border conflict. There was no sign of the Muslim visitors from Meerut, and it was only with some difficulty that I managed to

Photo 4: The desecratede grave of 'Sayyid sahib'.. Photographed in 1986.

rediscover the grave of "Sayyid sahib". It had been buried under a mound of dung cakes and shrubs. The other graves in the vicinity, which I had been informed belonged to the Sayyid's disciples, had

Photo 5 and 6: Desecratede graves in the waqf area. Photographed in 1986.

been overturned or partially covered by the ubiquitous dung cake huts. Upon tactful inquiry as to what had transpired in the area, I was told that at a panchayat meeting the Pradhan had voiced popular opinion when he had declared that "the Musalmans shall be thrown out of our village and community, it is our land which we shall defend with our blood". The ritual profanement of the locus-mundi of the shrine was the direct result. Another brave villager informed me of future plans: "we shall take apart the mosque brick by brick until nothing (of significance) remains for them". Although the villagers casually dismissed the mosque and grave as relatively new and insignificant, the seriousness with which they regarded the challenge to their primacy in the village was evident in their reactions to the attempts of the "Meerut-Muslims" to reconsecrate

Photo 7: Photograph of mosque in 1991. Compare with the one taken in 1985 to assess the intervening destruction.

the area and recall (unpleasant) memories of their past residence in the village. The Jat villagers had their version of the past, and this history had no place for Muslims, mosques, or *Sayyid al-Ḥujjāb*, all of whom in a microcosmic caricature of communal "national history" were branded as "foreigners" coveting the property of others. By 1991 only one of the pillars supporting the last cloister of the mosque had escaped destruction. There was little sign of the grave identified as belonging to "Sayyid-sahib"; it was virtually lost in the surrounding debris and vegetation.

Photo 8: Part of the khanaqah of Sayyid al-Hujjab with construction on roof.By 1991 the cloister on the far right housed a plastics factory.

The true irony behind this story of conflict over sacred space is that all the participants had misread their history. As Zafar Hasan had noted in his survey, the sacred shrine, the grave of Ma'rūf, was not located in the *waqf* area of the mosque at all, it was about four hundred metres distant in the Sayyid's *k͟hānaqah* which had been sold to Khem Chand sometime before 1913. According to Zafar Hasan this area had already been built upon and transformed by its residents, and the author had recommended to the Government of India that no money should be expended towards its preservation. An old Persian inscription memorialising Ma'rūf and praying for God's favour was removed from the structure and placed in the Delhi museum. But the outlines of the *k͟hānagah* were still visible when I visited the village. While the central structure had a massive house built around and over it, the lower walls were unmistakably of the Tug͟hluqid period. Several large cloisters extended from under the house and these were previously used as buffalo pens; in 1991 one of them housed a small factory.

Since the *khānaqah* was not a part of the *waqf* and therefore the scene of a latter day territorial conflict, it never became a part of the current episode in the making and re-making of the sacred history of *Sayyid al-Ḥujjāb*. This was in a sense most appropriate because the conflict had very little to do with Ma'rūf. In the fight over disputed land both the contesting parties took recourse to history; one who emphasised the presence of a sacred domain of the Sayyid, the other who slighted these claims by stating a primordial right of settlement to be protected from "foreign incursions".

That both the contestants were wrong in their separate reading of history is of marginal interest here. More interesting is the fact that the meaning and significance of what was "holy", "sacred", or "religious" were not fixed forever in time, but were subject to constant reinterpretation. As our experience with the daily world alters so too does the manner in which we interpret our past and define what we regard as sacred. Neither the past, nor our understanding of religion are ineffable "truths" whose meaning remains unaltered through the passage of time. While it is perhaps axiomatic to declare that history is subject to constant, sometimes contrary reinterpretations, it is a far more difficult proposition to convince people that the symbols of what they regard as sacred have undergone a similar process of dramatic redefinition over the years. Even if many of the symbols of what we regard as sacred today had their origin in early antiquity, with social and material changes through the passage of time, these same symbols often come to possess an alternate meaning and stand for completely different things. The elements through which the importance of places like Saidlajab or the "Ram Janambhoomi" for example, were resurrected had nothing to do with the original formulation that had attracted the religious sentiments of its residents. Together with other historical changes in their neighbourhood, the sacred was also redefined.

If we recognise that our religious beliefs cannot be attributed uncritically to "tradition" passed unchanged through time, we also need to bear the burden of the actions that stem from our religious beliefs more directly. After all, we are the ones that either make or acquiesce in the identification of what is sacred. If one of the consequences of our religious beliefs is a sense of hostility towards people of another religious denomination for what we believe are past wrongs, then complicitly we are like the "Meerut Muslims" or the Saidlajab villagers, or those individuals who carefully demolished Babur's mosque. The only way that we manage to assuage our conscience is by historicising our right to hate and wreak violence upon others even if we have not thrown the proverbial stone. Amongst everything else here, we are also functioning as very poor historians.

V
Postscript

Several years after writing this paper, in the summer of 2001, I visited the *waqf* area in the village once again. To my shock I discovered that the mosque had been completely demolished in

Photo 9: The *waqf* area in 2001. The raised mound in the centre was the site of the medieval mosque.

the intervening period. Not a trace remained of its rubble or of the graves. Barring a few stones from the roof, only a small mound in the centre of the open space indicated the site of the old mosque.

Together with the removal of the mosque and the attending graves, the village garbage dump and the dung cake huts had also vanished. The place was clean of thorn and scrub bushes; a few *kikar* trees remained to provide shelter on the raised area where the mosque had previously stood. The *waqf* land was now the village park; competitive volley-ball and neighbourhood cricket matches were in session on the occasions that I visited.

Despite the obvious prosperity and congestion that urbanisation had brought Saidlajab – corporate offices of Price-Waterhouse, mansions constructed by property developers – the *waqf* area was still vacant. But there were two new constructions there. The first was a tall light tower that illuminated the park with its halogen beams. A marble plaque memorialised its inauguration: none other than Sahib Singh Varma, the ex-Chief Minister of Delhi, had presided over the commemmoration of the medieval site into its present incarnation. Instead of the old Persian inscription acknowledging Ma'rūf, there was a new one heralding the present character of the park and the village. The villagers were grateful to the local MLA and Sahib Singh Varma for "help" in cleaning the park: "It was a dirty area, but it is now a wonderful park". Another more artless villager confessed, "With the removal of the ruins we have ensured that the Muslims will not come back to our village. We have wanted to do this for some years past."

The second construction in this area was, oddly enough, a new tomb encased in marble, with a small fence and a gate. This was in the approximate area of the demolished mosque. A dog was sleeping within the tomb precincts when I first visited the area on a summer afternoon. The second time was some months later in the evening when some village women were lighting candles by the shrine. I asked after the identity of the person buried in the tomb. No one knew. "It was the tomb of some old, pious person

Photo 10: The anonymous grave adjacent to the light tower. The memorial plaque thanking Sahib Singh Varma is at the base of the light tower..

that the women worship", I was told. "There are no Muslims in the village", another villager echoed, "and for the past fifteen years the panchayat has been trying to clear this area of the ruined mosque". Recently they had received permission from the court to do this (which court? they didn't say). It was then that the village women had started their worship at this grave. Who had built this grave? When was it built? No one knew. It was an odd grave, obviously new and incorrectly laid out, *NOT* in a north-south orientation as Muslim graves in India are, but on an east-west axis. A grave with no name and no history. The distance between *Sayyid al-Ḥujjāb* and the village of Saidlajab was complete. And with it was erased the complex history of movement and resettlement of people over centuries in a small village in Delhi.

Notes

1 A slightly different version was first published in *The India Magazine of her People and Culture* vol. 13 no. 10 (Sept. 1993).

2 For a short biography of *Sayyid al-Ḥujjāb* see Shams Sirāj 'Afīf, *Ta'rīkh-i Fīrūz Shāhī*, ed., Maulawi Wilayat Husain, (Calcutta: Bibliotheca Indica, 1882), pp. 445–451.

3 Ibid, pp. 448-9.

4 Ḥāmid ibn Faẓl Allāh Jamālī. *Siyar al-'Ārifīn*, (Delhi: Rizwi Press, 1893) and 'Abd al-Ḥaqq Muḥaddis Dehlawī, *Akhbār al-Akhyār*, Urdu trans., Mawlana Muhammad Fāzil, (Karachi: Madina Publishing Co., n.d.)

5 Abū'l Faẓl, *Ā'īn-i Akbarī*, trans. H. Blochmann, (Delhi: New Taj Office, 1989 reprint).

6 Yaḥyā ibn Aḥmad Sirhindī, *Ta'rīkh-i Mubārak Shāhī*, and Muḥammad Bihāmadkhānī, *Ta'rīkh-i Muḥammadī*, trans., Muhammad Zaki, (Aligarh: Centre for Advanced Study, 1972).

7 The events of these years have been discussed in Simon Digby, *War-Horse and Elephant in the Delhi Sultanate: a Study of Military Supplies*, (Karachi: Oxford University Press, 1971), pp. 74–82, and Gavin Hambly, "The Twilight of Tughluqid Delhi: Conflicting Strategies in a Disintegrating Imperium", in *Delhi Through the Ages: Essays in Urban History, Culture and Society*, (Delhi: Oxford University Press, 1986), pp. 45-62.

8 See Sirhindī, *Ta'rīkh-i Mubārak Shāhī*, pp. 145-54,

9 See Khwajah Ni'amat Allah, *Ta'rīkh-i Khān Jahānī wa Makhzan-i Afghānī*, edited S.M. Imam al-Din, (Dacca: Asiatic Society of Pakistan, 1960), vol. 1, p. 134. See also S.H. Hodivala, *Studies in Indo-Muslim History* (Bombay: Popular Book Depot, 1939), vol. 1, pp. 491-2 for doubts about reading Mehrauli in the text. Nirodbhusan Roy, *Niamatullah's History of the Afghans* (Santiniketan: Santiniketan Press, 1958), p. 30, fn 8, suggests Mewat as an alternative reading. This reading has some merit; Aḥmad Khān succeeded Bahādur Nahīr as the chieftain of Mewat. The village of Lādū Saray still has some extant monuments from the Sayyid dynasty in occupation by the villagers.

10 Abū'l Faẓl, *Ā'īn-i Akbarī*, vol. 3, pp. 291-2.

11 Cited in Irfan Habib, *Agrarian System of Mughal India (1556–1707)*, p. 342.

12 See the revised map adapted from Henry M. Elliot, *Memoirs on the History, Folklore and Distribution of the Races of the North-Western Provinces of India*, (London, 1869), in Joseph E. Schwartzberg, *A Historical Atlas of South Asia*, (Chicago: University of Chicago Press, 1978), p. 61, Plate VII.B.2.c.

13 M. Zafar Hasan, *Delhi Province: List of Muhammadan and Hindu Monuments* (Calcutta: Superintendent Government Printing, 1915–22, 4 vols.), vol. 3, pp. 121-3.

14 *Ibid*.

15 P.S. White (Surveyor), *Sketch of the Environs of Delhi, 1807*, reprint of the hand-drawn original, Surveyor General of India, 1989.

Naming

I like my name; it perplexes a lot of people. In chagrin, they keep asking me my “real” (caste) name so that they can then classify me socially and culturally. I like my children’s names: one is Shefali, the other is Sikandar. My nieces are Irfana and Saraswati-Nandini. Hindus and Muslims, all in the same family! Confusion compounded. I love it. But then we like this momentary anonymity; you have to make the effort to know us. Conventionally speaking, our names give away little.

The process of naming is rarely accidental and never trivial. To begin with, it involves considerable reflection and deliberate choice from a host of possible options. Even the retention (or dropping) of the family name is often deliberate in its intention to maintain (or obscure) a genealogical link. Names serve as identifiers, of who you are, and how others should know you within a larger social constellation. They can, therefore, be important indicators of the choices individuals make concerning group or ideological membership.

It is in acknowledgment of the evidence concerning social and cultural identities that a whole industry of historians study names.

Through a record of names kept at pilgrimage sites in medieval Europe, scholars reconstructed historical changes in the composition of families, matrimonial customs and inheritance patterns. Within the Islamic world, names have been studied as indices of religious and ideological identification, the process whereby individuals internalized new ideas or cosmologies over time, and were prepared to make a public acknowledgment of their beliefs.

The history of place-names is as interesting for what it has to tell us about the manner in which people chose to identify their own and others' areas of residence. In India, the region of Delhi has witnessed considerable demographic change through the years, and the city has come to incorporate neighbourhoods dating to different periods in the past. Some settlements are still known by their old names: Bhogal, Yusuf Sarai, Shaikh Sarai, Hauz Rani, Lado Sarai. Some abbreviation and corruption of old names has also taken place: Bagh-i Jud became Jod Bagh, Khirki masjid became Khirki, Badarpur Sarai became Badarpur, Malcha Mahal became Malcha Marg. Perhaps the most interesting process was that of renaming: Ghiyaspur was transformed into Nizamuddin; Siri into Shahpur Jat; Inderpat into Din Panah and then the vague Purana Qila; Kingsway into Raj Path; Queensway into Jan Path; and now Connaught Place has been renamed Rajiv and Indira Gandhi chowks.

If we recognize the implication of "naming" as a means of identifying properties which people believed rendered a place socially and culturally significant, then the swath of names from different historical epochs provides a unique entry point into the study of Delhi's history. Hauz Rani or more precisely Hauz-i Rani is interesting, because it is a later thirteenth century name for the site and carries the Perso-Arabic element Hauz, meaning reservoir, together with the Hindi title of Rani for queen. The "Rani" must have either constructed or patronized the reservoir before the Sultanate occupation of Delhi, sometime perhaps in the twelfth century. The thirteenth century chronicles do not provide us with the original name for this tank, but in incorporating "Rani" in their version of the name, the authors of the *Tabaqat-i Nasiri* and the *Fawa'id al-Fu'ad* honoured the memory of the Hindu queen. Subsequently, one of the southern gates of Muhammad Shah Tughluq's city of Jahanpanah (The Refuge of the World) was named the "Hauz-i Rani Gate". The city gate and the reservoir were significant enough as centres of local identification to provide the name Hauz Rani to the village settlement established in their neighbourhood. Areas which possessed local significance for a variety of different reasons – hauz's, bagh's, tombs, or sarais – and remained stable, if insulated centres of habitation over a long duration of time, sometimes kept their original names. Other areas were not so lucky: the Bagh-i Jasrath near the Hauz-i Rani, disappeared very early from historical and popular memory.

Names were also subject to corruption, especially when changes in the demographic composition of a region introduced new residents, who had little regard for the features believed to provide uniqueness to an area. Thus, for the fourteenth century disciples of Sayyid al-Hujjab, the presence of their teacher and his hospice on the Mehrauli-Badarpur road (near the Qutb minar), rendered the area significant. Their village was therefore named after him. When the original inhabitants were driven out by succeeding Mewatti and Jat migrants through the fifteenth to the twentieth centuries, the new residents had little attachment to the old shrine of the saint. The old structures were dismantled and built upon by the later Hindu migrants. In the absence of its original raison d'être, there was nothing to stop the name of the village from evolving from Sayyid al-Hujjab, to Sieud Lujab in 1807 and into its current version of Saidlajab. In a predictable denial of historical change, not merely did the villagers believe that they were the primordial residents, but that their version of the name of the village dated back into antiquity. Through this process of renaming and re-identification, new claims to lands and residence were legitimated. Sayyid al-Hujjab and the original residents of the hospice might just as well have never existed.

The corruption of an original place-name sometimes involved a variety of people not all of whom belonged to the local neighbourhood. The differing names applied to an area provide a valuable insight into the contradictory perceptions of people concerning the significance of the same site. A good example is Delhi's first Jami Masjid, better known today as the Qutb mosque. This mosque underwent construction and reconstruction at various times during the late twelfth, thirteenth and early fourteenth centuries. At the time of construction the mosque was uniformly described in the epigraphs and Persian chronicles as the "Masjid-i Jami" (the congregational mosque), and the Qutb was merely referred to as the "Minar". In the Tabaqat-i Nasiri, a chronicle written in the mid-thirteenth century, the Sultanate city of Delhi was called the "Qubbat al-Islam", or "the Sanctuary of Islam", a name which was perhaps also ascribed at a later time to the congregational mosque itself. During the eighteenth and nineteenth centuries, if not earlier, the minar was popularly referred to as "Qutb sahib ki lath", or the staff of the sufi saint Qutb al-Din Bakhtiyar Kaki buried in nearby Mehrauli. The popular cosmology in its fully developed form was wonderful. The sufi saint [Qutb al-Din] Bakhtiyar Kaki was a qutb, the axis, who protected the world from disorder, and this symbolism was articulated in the mosque which was the "sanctuary of Islam" where the minar itself represented the saint as the axis and stabilizer of the universe.

In the middle of the nineteenth century, scholars regarded much of this popular cosmology surrounding the Jami Masjid as superstitious nonsense and sought to discover the "real" name and meaning of the mosque. They concluded that the minaret was first constructed by Qutb al-Din Ai-Beg, and it should therefore be eponymously named after him. They argued that the reference to Qutb al-Din Bakhtiyar Kaki in the "Qutb sahib ki lath" was a corruption, originating from a false etymology. These scholars also concluded that "Quwwat al-Islam" or "the Might of Islam" was the authentic name of the mosque. From a purely positivistic perspective there was no evidence – epigraphic or documentary – that could support their conclusion. But in the interpretation of history, where Muslims were homogenized into a composite group, all uniformly militant, aggressive conquerors, proud of their iconoclasm, it seemed natural that Delhi's first congregational mosque should celebrate the "Might of Islam". Ironic as it may seem, it was scholars who corrupted the popular version of the name "Qubbat al-Islam" into "Quwwat al-Islam", all the while suggesting that it was their research which had discovered the original name of the mosque. It was a fateful christening, and supported by the weight of scholarly opinion, it was internalized as "truth" by subsequent generations of students. In this process of [re-]naming however, local residents played little role. In fact their understanding of the significance of the Jami Masjid was completely ignored. It was the manner in which a national history was being written, and the direction from which the events in its past were being interpreted, that determined not merely the meaning of the monument, but also its new name.

The end of colonial rule, partition, and the rapid growth in the size and population of the capital, also introduced a frenzy of naming. Post-partition migrants sought to preserve their identities in their Punjabi Baghs, Lajpat and Malaviya Nagars, Tagore and Chittaranjan Parks. New colonies of the upwardly mobile, with verdant visions of the future were established: Green Park, Mayfair Gardens, Panchsheel Park and Vasant Vihar, promised lands of plenty. Segregated communities identified their residences as Jamia or Ambedkar Nagars. These were names which reflected the often contradictory and competing "identifiers" which pulled the nation's citizens along different paths. As housing and residential committees searched the scriptures for auspicious names and Janakpuri, Greater Kailash and Saket were established, a different composite identity of the Hindu nation also received popular support.

In contrast to these trends, the state attempted to socialize its citizens along secular, socialist ideals. History and the media consolidated the image of a free India, the culmination of an epic "nationalist struggle", a transition through fire which united the people of the country, and transformed them all into patriots engaged in the making of their motherland. The euphoria of freedom was greeted by the symbolic removal of names from public sites which honoured erstwhile colonial masters. The process of renaming sites after an individual from Indian history was an expansive moment marked by considerable diversity in the selection of heroes: Asoka and Teen Murti, Aurangzeb and Shivaji were all accommodated within Delhi. In the post-independence xenophobic mood of searching for an indigenous identity and self-reliance, the historical lineage of the Indian nation had to erase the memory of "foreigners" who had subverted the country's independence.

The historical genealogy of the nation culminated with the country's latest heroes; the freedom fighters who had brought India to its "tryst with destiny". The ascriptive qualities of these nationalists coincided in one way or the other with the values which were seen to be central in the constitution of the new nation. These were people regarded as martyrs, one and all; they were principled fighters, either non-violent or eventually propelled to violence by grave injustice; they were constructive social workers, not merely dismantling an old regime but providing the moral inspiration for the construction of a new country; their private and public lives were models for all. Men were the responsible wage earners, public citizens and the patriarchs of the home; women were always supportive wives or even better, nourishing, protective mothers, the makers of the heroes of the infant nation. The iconography of India's past was mapped out in the streets of Delhi. If in the past Indians had been "led" to freedom by their heroes, their memory guided the residents of Delhi in the present. There was no 5th Avenue or Main Street in Delhi; instead you took Lala Lajpat Rai Road, into Zakir Husain Marg, took a left at Kasturba Gandhi Marg, and reached downtown.

Genealogies, however, are always prone to challenge and change. Much as the representation of India's ancient past came to be disputed by the fundamentalist Hindu nationalists in the present generation, more contemporary heroes also had to be celebrated to legitimize succession within the collateral lineages of the ruling elite. Until the 1960's there was no major controversy in the choice of the heroes of the "freedom struggle". The Congress party claimed a lineage which went back into 1885 and incorporated the largest chunk of heroes. And since the "good fight" was for a common cause, carefully screened "outsiders" were embraced as spiritual brothers within a polyheaded movement.

With the passage of time this was harder to accomplish, and certainly by 1969, with the split in the Congress and the imposition of Emergency, even the Congress party was utterly divided about who it regarded as its heroes. Today, despite the occasional massive electoral support, no political party represents the aspirations of the majority of Indians. This is not for want of trying. Huge political rallies, massive cardboard cutouts of political figures, sell the virtues of one or the other contender.

It was therefore intriguing when a political party with a bare majority in Parliament sought to alter the name of Delhi's central commercial complex in an election year. It was proposed by some members of the Congress (I) that Connaught Place named after the Duke of Connaught, should be renamed as the Rajiv and Indira chowks after the two prime ministers and the political party's self acknowledged, martyred idols. This attempt to gain electoral support was necessitated as the Congress (I) faced dissension and split within its ranks. The incumbent prime minister, Narasimha Rao argued consistently that the death of Rajiv Gandhi did not mark a hiatus in the rule of the Nehru-Gandhi family; the charisma of the original dynasts devolved upon the current leader and his supporters. The proximity to the ideals and the vision of Rajiv and Indira Gandhi motivated the "loyalist" faction of the Congress (I) to transform Connaught Place into a shrine immortalizing their beloved, martyred leaders. By exclusion, the dissidents within the party had no moral claims to leadership, a spiritual succession that ignored them as it traversed time into the glorious epoch of the freedom movement.

The Congress (I) also claimed that it was acting within the purest traditions of the freedom struggle in renaming Connaught Place and removing the vestiges of colonial heritage in the capital. But there were other residues of British presence in Delhi which it could have exorcised. The choice of Connaught Place as a site to make a "patriotic" statement was not accidental. In the post-liberation era of the nation's economy, this commercial complex, more so than India Gate or Rashtrapati Bhawan, is regarded as the centre of the city. The centrality of this area in the financial and social life of the metropolis, makes for a perfect shrine; the Indira Gandhi International Airport cannot compare. Once the commercial hub of the capital was named after Rajiv and Indira Gandhi, mother and son were fêted as the ultimate protagonists of the modern nation, the champions of a new economic order of liberalization which they helped to usher. The fact that the political party and the nation share a common parentage only confirms the Congress (I) credentials to be the historical representators of the nation through the different stages of its chronology. Although the irreverent may blaspheme and suggest that it is apt to name a bazaar after Congress politicians and their money making proclivities, succeeding generations of Delhites would be distant and ignorant of the actions of a dictator and the incompetence of her son. The Congress (I) banked upon this eventuality, and (to complete the awkward metaphor) saw it as a long term investment in the furtherance of their political interests.

The spasmodic reaction of seeking native identities is part and parcel of a larger representation of history indulged in by all nations.

The emergence of a nation implies the making of an imagined community hopefully contested over by differing ideologies. Connaught Place was one part of a larger theatre of New Delhi where the British dramatized their rituals of power, and rationalized their historical rights to lead the natives into a universe enlightened by their rule. Today, much like the village of Hauz Rani, the name Connaught Place has remained as a legacy after the disappearance of the power and symbolism of British colonialism. With the changes in the city of Delhi and the sky line of Connaught Place, the commercial complex bears little resemblance to the historical vision of the original constructors. The imposition of a new name upon Connaught Place is similar in many ways to the transformation of "Qubbat al-Islam" into "Quwwat al-Islam", a corruption of the name deliberately and authoritatively imposed upon the old mosque by outsiders. The new name, "Might of Islam", altered the symbolism of the monument and negated a history through which the local people had understood the mosque as the "Sanctuary of Islam". These were not "academic" revisions in nomenclature of limited arcane interest; it reconstituted a history of the past which validated the interpretation of two homogenous communities in a perpetually hostile relationship.

In the case of Connaught Place, even if the name survived through the years without corruption, it was enriched through accretion. A large number of people also call the commercial complex "C.P.", an acronym which had its origins in elite usage but which gradually gained a larger public currency. Like the village of Sayyid al-Hujjab known today as Saidlajab, "C.P." keeps its tenuous links with the past without carrying the historical baggage of the original name. Many residents of Delhi may regret this development, and feel that "C.P." (and Saidlajab) is a vulgarization of the original name. But at least it is part of a democratic tradition to arrive at consensual names for public spaces. In the middle ages a popular imagery had incorporated Delhi's old Jami Masjid within the saint Qutb al-Din Bakhtiyar Kaki's mystical domain and transformed the minaret into his staff, "Qutb sahib ki lath". The rejection of the popular name and cosmology was carried out without consideration of local, and if you wish, "vulgar" sensibilities – but with tragic consequences. It is precisely this subversion of the popular, democratic sentiment by the process of renaming through administrative fiat which is a colonial exercise. And it is not the presence of Connaught Place, but the renaming of the area as Rajiv and Indira Gandhi Chowks which marks the survival of colonial traditions of governance, the desperate attempts of an unstable government to gain a history by converting a public space into a shrine for its heroes.

Reflections on the Past and Present of two Sufi Shrines in Delhi

This chapter narrates the history of two Sufi shrines (*dargahs*) in South Delhi, one of which is in the modern neighbourhood of Saket while the other is less than a kilometre away in the adjacent Jahanpanah forest. The two *dargahs* are quite different from each other. The one in Saket, with several medieval structures on its site, is of Khwaja Maqbul Shah. Despite its obvious antiquity little is known about the saint buried on its premises. The second shrine, in the Jahanpanah forest, is of Khwaja Jalal al-Din Chishti Awliya, another anonymous Sufi saint, whose shrine emerged as a place of worship of some significance only in the 1980s. This is the smaller of the two shrines and although of recent vintage, it is extremely popular today, attracting pilgrims from towns as far away as Aligarh and Agra.

Both *dargahs* have been completely transformed in the last three decades. Narrating their history is instructive for the ways in which it recalls several themes that have populated the other chapters in this book. Perhaps the more familiar ones concerned the attempt to historicise the development of specific sites as centres of devotion, the role of human agencies in the constitution of the sacred and the spiritual and the ways in which changes in settlement patterns and social demography impacted on religious beliefs and the memories of old heritage sites. What was noticeable in most of the sites discussed in the previous chapters was the role of exogenous factors in enabling change: extraneous knowledge systems altered the meaning of the Qutb mosque; city planners could erase fragile memories of places like the Hauz-i Rani and new migrants and their histories displaced old residents and with them the pasts of the neighbourhood of Sayyid al-Hujjab. The rush of development and sycophantic political exigencies could also lead to renaming: through administrative fiat, Connaught Place became Rajiv and Indira Gandhi Chowks. But exogenous factors are only one set amongst many that altered the histories of Delhi's heritage sites.

In this paper, I would like to discuss how endogenous histories played a huge role in the different kinds of transformations that occurred in the Saket and Jahanpanah Sufi shrines (*dargah*s). Located in close proximity to each other but with very divergent histories, the two Sufi shrines also serve the very useful purpose of enlarging upon the inner complexities within Islam and in the context of global rhetoric, its modern, sometimes severely misunderstood manifestations. To understand the histories of these two *dargah*s within a larger context, I have therefore prefaced my narrative with a brief introduction on Islam, Sufism and grave shrines. These will help in highlighting significant aspects in the constitution and transformation of the two *dargahs* that are the specific concerns of this paper.

Islam, Sufism and grave shrines

In popular reflection and in a considerable swathe of academic writing, scholastic Islam and Sufism are often assigned contrasting characteristics. The faith and practice of scholastic Islam was framed by a textual interpretation of the *Qur'an*, its exegesis and juridical schools. The formation of these modes of interpretation and empirical methodologies for recovering authentic precedents, created a scriptural and juridical corpus of authoritative dimensions·

for many Muslims it defined their catechism of rituals and beliefs. And yet, they, and many others, could be drawn away from an exclusive dependence upon the "reasoning of the intellect" (*ilm al-aql*) towards Sufism and a more personalised devotion that appealed to the heart, based, as it was, upon the "science of love" (*ilm al-ishq*). These binary juxtapositions could collapse with surprising ease but they could also be the subject of rhetorical intervention and create exclusive, divisive boundaries within the Muslim community.

In Sufism the search for a union with a merciful, all-powerful, numinous God involved self abnegation, careful discipline and above all, a love of God that obliterated all other reality leaving the seeker, in turn, exalted at the prospect of close proximity with his/her beloved and sombre at the termination of that momentary ecstatic bliss. In its rejection of the material world and its transitory, external attractions, Sufi thought also placed a great deal of emphasis on intuition through which the devotee could access the inner hidden meaning of the revealed Word. Sufis did not deny the relevance of the scholastic theological and juridical traditions in their search for spiritual truth; most recognised their importance but as a fundamental point of reference, not a determining aspect of reality itself. Certainly their veneration of the *Qur'an* was unequivocal; God's Word was often the point of departure in their search for an inner, ultimate reality. And yet, rather than simply adhering to a system of rituals and beliefs, Sufis focused upon the intention that rituals served, foregrounding the inner, esoteric meanings in God's revelation accessible only to spiritual adepts.

Very rarely God bestowed a special grace upon select individuals, his friends (*awliya*), which allowed them the ability to comprehend this inner reality. For the larger part, however, some Muslims could hope to be guided to this truth through their spiritual preceptor, a *pir/Shaykh*. God's grace, in other words, could be accessed by Muslims but only through their *pirs*. Those who wanted to learn and follow the mystic path became *murids* or students of their teacher and lived in his hospice; others visited the master from time to time, listened to his sermons and remained a part of a lay congregation. Not all Sufi *pirs* had a large body of disciples or regularly hosted large congregational assemblies. Some preferred an ascetic life and the literary records of mystics seldom regarded the presence or absence of a large gathering of disciples as a reflection of a Shaykh's spiritual capacity.

The absence of a large congregation of disciples, however, could be somewhat of a disability in another way. Without disciples who maintained an oral or written account of their *pir* and his teachings, there was every possibility that the knowledge of his grace would fade from mortal memory. On the other hand, if a Sufi Shaykh had a large body of adherents, they would write about him, circulate his teachings and continue to venerate his grave after his death. Since the Shaykh's spiritual accomplishments were God given, His grace was not withdrawn at their master's death. Instead the *pir* then became God's bride and his disciples placed a veil, *chadar*, on his grave and commemorated his death anniversary as his wedding or *'urs*. Since the grace of the Shaykh lingered in his grave he was often referred to as *zinda-pir*, the immortal teacher, who continued to provide solace to his disciples.

Pilgrims would bring their problems and entreaties to his grave site which was usually managed by a descendent of the Shaykh. The whole experience of the pilgrimage was elevating and magical. Although he was no longer manifest physically, his spirit imbued the site. Visitors to the *dargah* listened to stories and songs (*qawwali*) extolling his life and, if they were lucky, he would appear in their dreams or intervene in magical ways in their lives and relieve them of their misfortunes. The caretaker of the *dargahs*, the *sajjada nishin*, would provide amulets and regulate the rituals and ceremonies associated with worship in the shrine. Death, in other words, did not terminate the experience of proximity to God that disciples felt when they visited their master. It is for this reason that so many of them chose to be buried in the vicinity of the shrine so that on the Day of Judgement their master could intervene favourably on their behalf with God.

Shrines had generations of servitors who kept up the ritual life of the *dargahs*, embellishing and expanding it with time. In fact, if one pretended to be a prosaic unbeliever for a moment – which would mean that you disregarded the charisma of the *zinda-pir* – it would not be difficult to conclude that the prosperity of a shrine was vitally dependent upon the entrepreneurial and management skills of its caretakers. Hence, it would follow that Shaykhs who did not possess a large congregation of followers were at somewhat of a disadvantage in that their graves did not immediately become centres of veneration. And yet, fickle memories notwithstanding, some of these graves were rediscovered by disciples many years later; the *zinda-pir* – so we are told – were merely waiting for the right moment to reveal their charisma and attract disciples to their grave sites.

Although the worship at *dargahs* was as much a part of Sufi practice as the performance of *sama'* (better known today as *qawwali* or invocatory singing), all Sufis were not equally comfortable with these practices. Even within Sufism there were multiple strands and if they shared a common belief it would be in a greater reality in this universe hidden from the vision of ordinary mortals which could be accessed only through a carefully cultivated control of the individual's base, sensory impulses. The path (*tariqa*) to this reality varied amongst Sufis: it could be through ecstatic rituals, poetry, music or the intervention of a "friend of God". The *pir* was venerated because of who he was, himself (and, more rarely, herself): a special individual who mediated God into the lives of his disciples during his lifetime and beyond. But even if shrine worship could be accommodated within Sufism there was, and still is, a great deal of ambiguity attached to its practice amongst many sections of Muslims.

Shi'i Muslims, for example, often find it difficult to accept not just shrine worship, but Sufism in general. The Shi'a believe that only 'Ali and his descendents have access to hidden, divine knowledge – an exclusive knowledge gained through their genealogical relationship with the Prophet. The claims of Sufi Shaykhs to a similar kind of access to knowledge could not be countenanced. And yet, amongst Shia communities today grave shrines of Sayyids, descendents of the Prophet, are centres of worship. The genealogical link with Muhammad and 'Ali allows for the transmission of esoteric knowledge of a form not very different from Sufism.

Within Sunni Islam the attitude to Sufism is equally varied. At one extreme were some jurists and theologians, who believed in the *Qur'an* and the traditions of the Prophet according to a very precise, empirically based interpretation of definitive texts. Their scholastic inclinations left them with little patience with Sufi claims to *nur-i batin*, or an inner light that guided mystics in their search for truth and reality. There were other jurists and scholars, however, who could adjust their scholarly commitments with a mystical inclination without any sense of contradiction whatsoever. In this they were joined by many Sufis who even while they pursued their mystic inclinations also took scholastic interpretations of law and theology very seriously. But there were also other Sufis who were extremely critical of scriptural exegesis. They disliked *'ilm al-aql* and scholars whose textual learning made it difficult for Muslims to go beyond books and the material world in search of true knowledge. As one early fourteenth century Sufi Shaykh put it, "scholars are like children who are dragged to school to learn their alphabets. They manage to learn their *alif, be, pe,* but they can never grasp the true meaning of these letters."

Despite the claims and counter-claim made by one or the other, none of these groups exclusively spoke for Islam. Unlike Christianity, Islam does not possess a Church that regulated dogma and belief or had the authority to enunciate orthodoxy. As a result, its multiple strands could claim legitimacy by virtue of their ascription to its central doctrines that related, for example, to God's unity or the status of Muhammad as the last of the Prophets. This did not mean that claims for authoritative interpretation of dogma were not made; these interventions did happen from time to time and they were sometimes very intrusive and violent. But as we have already noted in the earlier chapter on the Qutb, these interventions were always open to challenge and contestation. Resistance to those who espoused a self-professed orthodoxy created some of Islam's most venerable heroes and martyrs – the jurist Ibn Hanbal, for example, or the Sufi al-Hallaj.

It was the dialectic between its multiple strands that has historically made Islam such a dynamic, vibrant religion of enduring attraction to people of diverse backgrounds throughout the world. And yet, quite paradoxically, it is not the multiplicity or the dialogue within Islam that is foregrounded in the global media today; instead it is a combative, ultra-nationalist, conservative, doctrinal Islam that gains the greatest reportage. Sufi shrines claim little attention and if they do, in South Asia at least, they are not treated as an integral part of Islam but the product of miscegenation – the vernacularisation of a pristine [foreign] Islam as it came into contact with the indigenous cultures of the Indian subcontinent. Rather than interpreting it as a part of the historical "venture of Islam", as one historian put it, sufi shrines are decontextualised from the larger history of Islam and interpreted as a phenomenon of special uniqueness in South Asia providing, therefore, no theoretical insights with which we can understand the constitution of the religion itself. As I discuss the history of the two *dargahs* in South Delhi, I hope my narrative will also unravel the complex relationship between Sufism, Sufi shrines and Islam and the fate of the religion in contemporary India where global and indigenous historical processes have homogenised its lived multiplicities into a rounded, monolithic community. As a beginning, let us take a look at the shrine in Saket more closely.

The dargah of Khwaja Maqbul Shah in Saket

As you drive into the modern suburb of Saket in South Delhi today and negotiate your way through its choked traffic, past the capital's largest shopping mall and a five star hotel it is almost impossible to recall the area as it was in the 1970s: mustard fields, sparse tree coverage, a lonely road, no traffic or pedestrians, the distant *chug-chug* of a tube-well interspersed with the mooing of ambling cattle and the tinkle of their bells. Without electricity, night fell rapidly on the area and the glow of dispersed, solitary kerosene lamps, the sound of crickets in the echoing silence only accentuated the enveloping darkness and sense of loneliness.

On one of the two main roads entering Saket was a huge pipal tree; you noticed it before you espied the ruined wall of the mosque over which it towered. Other than its obvious age the mosque was unimpressive. It was what is called a *qanati masjid*, a kind, common during the Lodi period in the fifteenth and sixteenth centuries. At their inception, *qanati masjids* might have been perambulatory tent-mosques; the term *qanat* meaning canvas or tent. In their sedentary, stone and mortar incarnations, these mosques were constructed on a small pedestal where the only significant feature was the western *qibla* wall. Sometimes, as in the mosque in Saket, the remnants of a small courtyard enclosed by low walls would still be visible. The Saket *qanati masjid* was approximately fifteen metres wide and twenty-five metres deep.

Only the archaeologically minded would notice these details however. The few people who visited the ruined mosque precincts in the 1970s did not go there to read their prayers and certainly out of no antiquarian delight. They went to visit a small brick shed with an asbestos roof within the courtyard of the mosque. Inside this unplastered shed was a grave with a green *chadar*. This was the grave of Khwaja Maqbul Shah. Some flowers were strewn on the *chadar* and stubs of incense sticks littered the head of the grave. Near the shed were a few other unmarked and unadorned graves. When I first noticed the ruined mosque wall and grave in 1975 there was no placard identifying the grave nor was there anything immediately visible in the mosque area to stop someone like me, a rare passer-by, to investigate and take another look.

I was back in a relatively more urbanised Saket in 1983, this time as an unemployed graduate student in dire need of divine

Photo 1. Grave of Khwaja Maqbul Shah.

intervention to improve my job prospects. My wife and I were taken to the grave in the asbestos roofed shed by my mother-in-law, a more devout soul than us, and we offered flowers and sweets at the grave (photograph 1). By this time I knew somewhat more about Islam, the Delhi Sultanate and the geography of the city and I wanted to investigate the *qanati masjid* somewhat more closely as a part of the architectural landscape of an area outside the Sultanate cities

Photo 2. Baba Abdul Wali Shah, the servitor of the shrine.

of *Dihli-i kuhna* and *Jahanpanah*. I went back to visit the mosque and study its precincts which is when I met Abdul Wali Shah, the servitor of the shrine (photograph 2).

Abdul Wali Shah lived in a cluster of huts together with his extended family adjacent to the mosque. He was an old man, perhaps in his late seventies and was simply called "Baba" by all relatives and visitors. He would greet me, send one of his scampering grand-children to fetch tea and we would sit and chat on one of the string-cots under the *pipal* tree.

"Chat" is perhaps too strong a word to describe our exchanges because Baba Wali Shah was quite inarticulate. It is not that he was given to long silences; he would talk, his sentences prefaced by a gargle, his thoughts would taper off and he would start sentences several times over, spit constantly, stop and smile suddenly as if his thoughts had miraculously beamed themselves into your head. "Chatting" was a frustrating exercise if you were engaged, as I was, in discovering the history of the saint buried in the shed. All I was told was that his name was Khwaja Maqbul Shah and that he belonged to the time of Sultan Mahmud of Ghazni, in the early eleventh century. The historical contextualisation was quite accidental. As I later discovered, of all the pre-Mughal rulers, the Baba was only familiar with the name of Mahmud of Ghazni; quite surprisingly he knew nothing else about the Sultan or his iconoclastic activities. Baba Wali Shah was more interested in underlining the fact that he was a direct descendent of Maqbul Shah and that I should visit the ruin just behind the mosque. Here I followed his direction, and discovered the ruins of a wonderful stepped well (*baoli*), hidden from the mosque but barely fifteen metres to its east.

Although it was also in ruins, the *baoli* was clearly much larger and grander in its architectural conceptualisation than the mosque. It was placed in a north-south orientation with a wide bank of steps on the south leading down to the tank. Its walls were crumbling and its base was filled with debris and silt (photograph 3). There was enough of the wall and arches still extant to confirm that it could be dated, like the mosque, to the fifteenth-sixteenth century Lodi period. I was delighted to discover the *baoli* because it confirmed the diligence with which water resources in the South Delhi plain had been harvested from the thirteenth through the

Photo 3. The Baoli, taken from the north.

sixteenth centuries. The *baoli* together with the *Hauz-i Rani* and the Satpula sluice gate dam on the Jahanpanah city wall, tapped the rivulent that overflowed from the "King's reservoir", *Hauz-i Sultani*, otherwise known as *Shamsi Talab* today, just south of the Qutb, before it meandered north to join the Yamuna, beyond Nizamuddin and Humayun's tomb. In contrast to the frequent remarks about bad planning leading to a dearth of water in the Sultanate cities of Delhi, public authorities and local residents in the middle ages had invested considerable wealth in harvesting the considerable water discharge of the seasonal streams from the western hills of the Delhi plain. The *baoli* in the Maqbul Shah shrine was another evidence of this phenomenon.

I continued to visit Baba Wali Shah through the 1980s during which time the first signs of change in the *dargah* precincts became visible. Although the quality of our conversations was still frustrating, I had shifted from my original investigative empirical mode to one that studied his interaction with visitors to the grave shrine. Through the decade the number and social background of the visitors to the *dargah* had altered. It had started with the arrival of some Afghan refugees in the Saket colony after the Soviet invasion. These refugees were in search of a mosque in the convenient vicinity of Saket and, like many others, they had also noticed the old *qanati masjid*. In the meantime its premises had been swept clean and the *qibla* wall white-washed. Slowly a small gathering of Muslims would read the Friday prayers every week here. Their presence also attracted Muslim residents from the Hauz Rani village and although it had its own small mosque a trickle also started coming to the *qanati masjid*. I did not know this at that time but many of these developments coincided with the takeover of the mosque by the Delhi Waqf Board in 1979. This organisation funded the maintenance and administration of select Muslim religious centres in the Delhi region. They were the ones who had the *qibla* wall whitewashed.

None of these developments had displaced the position of Baba Wali Shah and his family as descendents and servitors of Maqbul Shah's shrine. In fact the arrival of larger number of people at the mosque could have theoretically helped in revitalising the *dargah* as well. Instead there was tension in the air. The visitors to the mosque often came and conversed with the Baba; more appropriately, *tried* to converse with him. His poor communication skills were underlined by the presence of a young man who, as the *imam* of the mosque, led its small congregation of worshippers into prayer. He was a self confident young man, scrubbed and clean, always dressed in a spotless, starched kurta-pyjama, passionate and articulate with claims to being a *hafiz*, a person who had memorised the *Qur'an*. This young man was often present when people came to converse with the indolent, hukka chugging Baba. Baba Wali Shah was the butt of interminable teasing: "tell the visitors some grand stories about Maqbul Shah" the *imam* would chortle, "regale them with stories about how he made his cot fly and made the wall move". These remarks would be followed by much back slapping and sniggers amongst the *imam's* intimates. The poor Baba would clear his throat, spit and explode, "yes, it is true he had miraculous powers, he did all that". But Wali Shah had no magical tales, no parables of epic proportions, nothing through which he could communicate Maqbul Shah's spiritual charisma to his audience. In his inability to touch an emotional chord with his visitors it was the *zinda-pir* who hardly appeared alive. In his ability to gain adherents for the *dargah*, the Baba was losing the battle with the mosque and its *imam*. It was not a scene that I enjoyed and I stopped going to the shrine.

Although I stayed away for nearly a decade, I drove or walked by the mosque regularly and could notice how change was sweeping the place. There was to begin with rapid construction on the site of the mosque. Its *qibla* wall was encased in fresh plaster and then extended until it disappeared completely within a resplendent, high ceilinged cloister (see photograph 4 and 5). A new towering entrance to the mosque with a large dome (see photograph 6) was in the process of being constructed and a large hoarding declared that the structure was the congregational mosque, Jama Masjid, of the dargah of Maqbul Chishti. Since the hoarding still identified the place as a *dargah*, I thought of the construction as largely cosmetic developments – but I could not have been more wrong (see photograph 7).

I revisited the *dargah* with some students in 1998. In the interim Baba Wali Shah had passed away. His descendents still resided on the premises but their access to the mosque was blocked; they resided in small rooms outside its walls. I asked after the new servitor of the shrine and met with blank stares. Instead I was directed to the new *imam* of the mosque, Maulana Shihabuddin. This was not the entrepreneurial young man that I knew from my past visits. Maulana Shihabuddin was appointed by the Waqf board and he refused to talk with me. I was directed instead to the head of the Muslim community of the Hauz Rani village, Pradhan Haji Muhammad Jathariya. The mosque was now under his jurisdiction. Nobody spoke of the *zinda-pir* Khwaja Maqbul Shah anymore; the mosque had hegemonised the entire

Photo 4. The new cloister encasing the qibla wall of the mosque.

Photo 5. Northern wall of the mosque with part of the original compound. The madrasa is in the small rooms in the right corner of the photograph.

Photo 6. The new entrance to the mosque.

Photo 7. The hoarding on the entrance to the mosque.

premises. Khwaja Maqbul Shah's name adorned the hoarding at the entrance to the mosque but inside his presence was palpably absent.

Past tensions between the *imam* and the Baba, the scale and quality of the ongoing construction within the mosque precincts had portended these trends but I was unprepared for their enormity. The grave of Khwaja Maqbul Shah received an honoured space within the cloister of the mosque. It was now renovated with screens and

Photo 8. he renovated grave of Maqbul Shah now inside the mosque.

decorated tiles, but significantly it lacked a *chadar*, the sign that would declare that it was the resting place of a *pir* who was a bride of Allah (see photograph 8). Now it was the grave of just any other eminent Muslim. Khwaja Maqbul Shah was stripped of his Sufi identity; the *zinda pir* had finally passed away. My old friend, Baba Wali Shah was also buried in the mosque with only the humbleness of the grave distinguishing him from his *pir* (see photograph 9).

The Sufi character of the old shrine, the quality that had attracted my mother-in-law to seek his blessing and intervention for her family were no longer present. Instead construction continued in

Photo 9. Grave of Baba Abdul Wali Shah in the courtyard of the mosque.

the mosque and each piece of stone and mortar consolidated the new scholastic, ritualistic incarnation of Islam within the old shrine premises. A school, *madrasa*, for young children was constructed on the side of the mosque (see photograph 5) and in the afternoons you would find young children in their ubiquitous kurta-pyjamas and skull-caps hunched over their slates, chanting rhythmically, swaying back and forth, trying to memorise their texts. The biggest shock occurred when I went to search for the *baoli*. It had vanished – completely disappeared! The huge stepped well was filled in with earth and only bits of forlorn walls on its south-east edge remained of the old grand structure (see photograph 10). Descendents of Baba Wali Shah who had rooms not far away from this area, informed me of the Pradhan's plans to build a large *madrasah* for *Qur'an* instruction. There was no sorrow in their voices only an excitement at the prospect of change and progress: an old ruin, which only accumulated garbage, had given way – what new, flamboyant building would come up in its stead?

Photo 10. The vanished baoli. Compare with photograph 3.

It was not just the architectural environment that had altered in the *dargah*, the mood of the people and the reasons why they visited it had also changed. Readers may notice the strange absence of people in the photographs illustrating this shrine. After my early "tourist" photographs, I did not want to take my camera during my conversations with the Baba and introduce what I thought might be an alienating dimension to our informal relationship. Nor did I think at that time that this world would slip away so quickly and hence felt little urgency to document it. When I went back in the late 1990s and noticed the changes, I was keen on recording my observations but felt constrained to do so because of the visible hostility that came my way. Whereas in the past my religious identity was not a subject of concern to anyone in the *dargah*, the new mosque and its administrators were extremely conscious that this was a space within which Islam was taught and reproduced. It had to be protected from a variety of different threats and I was one of them.

This was the 1990s, the Babri masjid and the Bombay riots were not distant memories. Even more immediate were developments closer to home: the "usurpation" of the common-lands of the Hauz Rani villagers by the D.D.A. Saket Sports Complex, the resplendent renovation of a Sanathan Dharma temple down the street from the mosque, a renovation that had the support of the local Resident Associations who prevailed upon city authorities to rename Saket's

Photo 11. Looking South from the courtyard of the mosque, the five-star hotel.

main street "Mandir Marg". The sense of being besieged was complete when the Marriott, Saket's lone five-star hotel, arrived

Photo 12. Looking east from the mosque, construction activity in the shopping mall.

as the immediate neighbour of the mosque and construction in the city's largest shopping mall commenced in earnest just behind the old *baoli* (see photographs 11 and 12). If the Baba's fanciful stories carried the threat of lulling the faithful into believing in the miraculous power of saints and their supernatural abilities to intervene in the lives of disciples, the hotel and the mall were the devil's attempts at tempting Muslims into immoral consumption and promiscuous life styles. The new mosque was the bastion of Islam that protected the community from the influence of these pernicious ideologies. Haji Muhammad Jathariyya, the Pradhan who had managed the mosque from its early construction years, guarded his achievements very jealously. He enforced strict discipline within the mosque precincts – comportment and speech were policed, conservative dress and gender discrimination were enforced. A heathen such as I, with a troop of young students – young adults of both genders, casually dressed and obviously having a good time in each other's company – spelled trouble. I was accosted, harangued and shooed away. The mosque was for Muslims, we were told, and we had no business there.

This was a conservative, defensive, ghettoised face of Islam familiar to the students thanks to the media coverage after 9/11. The students had not witnessed the other traditions of Islam that had occupied the same site just over a decade ago or had any knowledge of the historical interventions and debates that had led to the eventual success of the present version. Narrating its past was therefore important to provide the present with some context and to disturb the many stereotypes that they carried about Islam.

But the unfolding history of Khwaja Maqbul Shah's mosque has a final bittersweet twist to it. As it happened, Pradhan Haji Muhammad Jathariya died in 2006 and when I visited the mosque in 2007 no successor had as yet been appointed as a replacement. The hiatus, however, opened possibilities of discourse absent before. I had arrived there with the usual retinue of students but this time no one harangued us and the swarm of curious kids from the *madrasa* who surrounded us were shooed away. In fact, I had a very cordial conversation with a butcher who went so far as to advise me to ignore the maulvis if they were to harass us. "The mosque", he said, "is a place of worship to God and everyone who comes here with respect is welcome". The butcher had a shop in Saket and did not look at the expanding commercial opportunities in the neighbourhood with the abhorrence characteristic of the Haji. Without jeopardising the dignity of his religion he held out the possibilities of future developments in the mosque precincts that were not utterly decontextualised from their environs. But it was the mosque, not the *dargah* under the *papal* tree that was the face of Islam to the residents and visitors to Saket. And the hints of change notwithstanding, the mosque on Saket's Mandir Marg remained distant and foreboding.

The shrine of Jalal al-Din Chishti Awliya in the Jahanpanah forest

Less than a kilometre from Saket is a long, narrow stretch of greenery nearly five kilometres long that starts at the village of Chiragh Dilli and curves towards the medieval fort of Tughluqabad. This is the Jahanpanah forest park with picnic areas interspersed with large idyllic wooded sections. I was bicycling through the forest with my daughter on a winter evening in 1984 when we chanced upon a grave-shrine. I was informed subsequently that this was the shrine of Jalal al-Din Chishti Awliya.

Quite in contrast to the shrine of Khwaja Maqbul Shah this was clearly not a shrine of any antiquity. All it consisted of was a grave whose features were shrouded by a *chadar*. The grave rested on a recently constructed platform with an asbestos roof supported by concrete pillars. The *chadar* covering the grave was a heavy fabric,

Photo 13. 1984 photograph of the grave of Khwaja Jalal al-Din Chishti.

bright green in colour with sequin embroidery at the edges. Over the grave was an awning of the same colour as the *chadar* but of a lighter material and much richer in its ornamentation. Streamers hung from the awning and the asbestos roof as did stars and translucent paper globes in which oil lamps could be lit at night. The bright decorations and the awning attracted the gaze of visitors to

Photo 14. 1984 photograph of the grave and its open wooded environs.

Photo 15. 1984 photograph of the grave with the servitor Muhammad Yaqub.

the shrine giving it the appearance of a shining jewel in the midst of wild greenery (see photographs 13, 14 and 15).

A serious, devout looking man sat at the foot of the grave. He introduced himself as Muhammad Yaqub Chishti, the servitor (*sajjada nishin*) of the shrine of Jalal al-Din Chishti Awliya. As far as I could make out the tomb did not have a gravestone and I asked him how he knew that Jalal al-Din was buried here and what he knew about the saint. Yaqub told me that Jalal al-Din was an Awliya, a friend of God, who had lived centuries ago. He had appeared to Yaqub in a dream and directed him to his grave. Yaqub was instructed to clean the site and make it a site of pilgrimage. The *zinda-pir* was awakening from his slumber and calling his disciples to him.

Quite in contrast to Baba Wali Shah, Yaqub was a born storyteller. He explained how his dream was like watching a show on television, a slowly unfolding story of Jalal al-Din's life and identification of his family members. They were all buried in the vicinity of the *pir's* tomb: "His brother is buried under the tree over there, the grave of another is under the bush…they are all here, keeping Awliya sahib company". I asked if Yaqub had any explanation why Jalal al-Din Chishti might have chosen him as his deputy. Yaqub suggested it must be because he was a distant descendant; the two did share the same last name – Chishti. This surname evoked powerful sentiments within Muslim circles in north India referring as it did to the great spiritual lineage founded by Mu'in al-Chishti at Ajmer, with luminaries like Bakhtiyar Kaki, Baba Farid and Nizam al-Din Awliya as some of its greatest *pirs*. This was a resplendent lineage to tap into and it was reflective of Yaqub's general facility at making a lingering impression.

Yaqub's demeanour, for example, was always kind, in an avuncular, contemplative and serious kind of way. He did not try to appear as your friend, but as a reflective guide with whom you could share your problems. Nor did he have long conversations with pilgrims. He listened attentively, summarised their grievances effectively and had quick, decisive solutions to offer. He did not ignore anyone, nor did he linger in his ministration over them. He was solicitous of women and their problems, always very correct and behaved like a condescending patriarch. On Fridays, he would give a brief sermon which would concern itself with general material problems faced by his audience – increasing prices, difficulties in managing family budgets, inter-personal conflicts within the household – and would provide resolutions that would paraphrase the teachings of Jalal al-Din Chishti Awliya. The grace of the saint touched the audience through his servitor and the audience was always still and attentive as they listened to his discourse. This was important because only Yaqub was privy to Jalal al-Din's teachings which had appeared in his dreams. Pilgrims, should they have wanted, did not have recourse to any text.

Yaqub had ambitions for the *dargah* and his ministry. Although only recently summoned by his *pir*, he was completely pledged to his calling. He would personally sweep the pedestal of the grave and water the earth around the shrine twice a day. He planned on starting the *'urs* celebrations in the near future with *qawwali* and food offerings. And eventually he planned to publish a compilation of the *pir's* teachings. Much as the *imam* had been in the Saket mosque, it was the servitor of the Sufi shrine in the Jahanpanah forest that was the entrepreneur.

More than the rudimentary *dargah*, the shrine's natural environs attracted me back periodically. Within a couple of years one could notice the gradual appearance of the formal trappings of a Sufi shrine in the forest. An additional asbestos shelter was constructed to the west of the grave. Pilgrims could shelter from the elements as they conversed with their *zinda-pir*. There was no formal mosque or *qibla* wall for the longest time but prayer carpets would be spread at the appropriate time for *namaz*. There was no water in the shrine so clay pots first appeared and eventually large prefabricated water tanks so that worshippers could perform their ablutions, *wuzu*, before prayer. Yaqub could be quite inventive.

He stuck to his promise of starting the *'urs* celebration (the death/marriage anniversary) of the saint. I remember in 1986, when the shrine was still receiving water in clay pots, Yaqub did not have the means to invite professional *qawwals* (singers) for the *'urs*. He compromised and brought cassettes of *qawwali* music and the forest echoed with their serenades played off his small Sony three-in-one.

The people who visited the shrine for the auspicious *'urs* celebrations were from the neighbouring colonies: Sheikhsarai, Ambedkar Nagar, Govindpuri, all largely poor and lower middle-class colonies. Yaqub was quite blunt about the composition of his audience: "it is the poor who are troubled and need sustenance," he said, "the value of true belief has not yet penetrated the rich residents of Saket and Masjid Moth". Simple as the preparation for the *'urs* might have been, there was no gainsaying the quality of emotion generated on the day. A woman from Sheikhsarai dashed up to the grave in an agitated manner and started weeping and banging her head on the pedestal: "why have you deserted me Baba," she wailed, before bursting into tears again. Yaqub remained impassive and still through the whole event and when I asked why he did not intervene, he explained that she was a *diwani*, lost in ecstasy and love, and should not be interfered with. Counselling could wait till when she was sober.

I could never discover any details about Yaqub's background. He was always very conscious about his position and stature which did not brook intimacy. But what was amazing about his teaching and comportment was the ease with which he imported stock Sufi ideas into his discourse. Take dreams, for example, which were of such significance to him in his discovery of his *pir's* tomb. To a sceptic this would be a figment of his imagination, credible only, it might seem, to the exceptionally simple-minded. But in Sufism dreams are the means by which the subconscious guides the dreamer towards reality. There are countless stories in Sufi texts on how *pirs* warned their disciples of impending danger, of instructions that disciples received subliminally. Dreams were a part of the

Sufi *nur-i batin*, the hidden knowledge that mystic novices had to actualise in their search for true knowledge. In the case of Yaqub, this intuitive capacity had been activated by his *pir* the moment he called him to his service. Yaqub was also sensible to the binarism in Sufism – the sense of ecstatic bliss that came when the faithful felt close to God/Reality and the sense of loss as withdrawal from that momentary union set in. It was sensitively apparent in his treatment of the *diwani* pilgrim demanding proximity with her *pir*. Finally, it was also apparent in the strong emphasis that Yaqub placed upon the formal ritual of daily prayer. To those uninitiated into Sufism *namaz* rarely goes beyond the boundaries of standing witness to the unity of God, acknowledging that all believers belong to one community equal in the eyes of their Maker, and submitting to His Word and final judgement. But the Sufis who find hidden meanings in the *Qur'an*, also discover in the act of praying a powerful, enabling moment when they could gain proximity to God, absolve themselves of sin, gain favour and, depending upon their choice of chapter and verse, a remedy for specific afflictions. Like the old *qanati masjid* in the *dargah* of Khwaja Maqbul Shah in Saket, all Sufi shrines have a mosque on their premises where the faithful could read their prayers. Yaqub had not missed the significance of this ritual and right from the very beginning he tried to ensure that Jalal al-Din's shrine had provisions for the reading of *namaz*. This included arranging for prayer carpets, water in earthen pots for ritual ablutions before prayer and the ambition to eventually construct a small mosque with a proper *qibla*.

It would be some years before all of this could be put into place – and not all of it happened in Yaqub's lifetime. He passed away prematurely, I am not sure when exactly, because I did not visit the shrine through the 1990s. During the intervening period, however, I would drive by the Jahanpanah forest and notice signs of uninterrupted prosperity in the *dargah*: large hoardings had started appearing, advertising the shrine and the annual *'urs* event (see photograph 16).

Photo 16. Advertisement of the ‘urs on the Jahanpanah forest wall.

Photo 17. Muhammad Irfan the new servitor of the shrine.

Photo 18. The approach to the shrine with the prefabricated water tank.

Yaqub's ambitions for the shrine were coming true. After his death, his young son Muhammad Irfan became the next servitor of the shrine (see photograph 17). He was every bit as efficient and impressive as his father. When I went back in 2005 it was during *Ramazan*. A huge congregation had gathered at the shrine in the evening. After circumambulating Jalal al-Din Chishti's grave, his disciples gathered at the small mosque where a decade ago Yaqub had spread prayer mats for *namaz*. After prayer all the worshippers partook in a community meal and broke their fast. Very graciously and without any reservation whatsoever they invited me to join them in a meal of *pulao* and curds.

In 2007 I visited the shrine again a day after the *'urs* celebration. Although the festivities were over, streamers still decorated the entry to the *dargah* (see photograph 18) and it carried an expansive, festive air. There was no need for Yaqub's three-in-one; they had live *qawwali* now. The central shrine now had a dome with *Qur'anic* verses inscribed on it (see photograph 19). Verandahs extended out from the grave shrine on all sides but it was still not large

Photo 19. Qur'anic verses decorate the new dome over Jalal al-Din Chishti. More recently these have given way to mirror inlay.

enough to hold the crowd of diverse people coming from distant areas and not just Delhi. Their clothes and deportment suggested their mixed social backgrounds; these were not all poor or lower middle-class pilgrims. I tried to take a photograph of the decorations inside the main hall. It inadvertently captures how the fervour of the *'urs* celebration had not dissipated the day after the event: excitement was still in the air and the pushing and shoving of the crowd shook my camera (see photograph 20). Despite all the changes the shrine was still a beautiful place, with twinkling lights encased in a green wilderness (see photograph 21). Cats and dogs frolicked in its premises and nobody gave them another glance. As

Photo 20. 2007 photograph of the shrine taken the day after the 'urs.

in Yaqub's lifetime it had made careful attempts to integrate with its habitat. The disciples would sprinkle flour mixed with sugar at the foot of the trees – for the ants or as an offering to the kinsmen of Jalal al-Din Chishti, I could not be sure.

Within twenty years, the father and son had turned an ordinary grave in the wilderness into a flourishing Sufi shrine. I marvelled at their management skills where prosperity and success was also related to their carefully calibrated reading of Sufism and

Photo 21. Green wilderness still sorrounds the shrine.

scholastic Islam. The combination of these elements became somewhat more apparent as the shrine flourished and developed an institutionalised regimen. When I had talked with Yaqub in 1986 I had asked him whether his ministry at Jalal al-Din's grave had created any controversy – if he had faced opposition from anyone. I had deliberately left the question open-ended wondering if he would seize the opportunity to complain of the park administrators, the municipality or harassment from the local police constables. Yaqub did not rise to the bait. In fact, he made no reference to the civic administration of the city at all and spoke, instead, of the general hostility of the Deobandis and the Barelavis towards Sufi shrines. Yaqub was alluding to the great educational institutions of religious learning at Deoband and Bareli where jurisprudence, theology and grammar was imparted to aspiring scholars. In these institutions a scriptural, textual version of Islam is taught and many of its graduates are the leading scholars, theologians and jurists in the subcontinent today. In their attempts to reform Islam they are often hostile and critical of what they regard as the superstitious innovations in practice amongst "uneducated" Muslims. It was their ignorance, they believed, that promoted faith in amulets to ward of evil, miraculous stories of Sufi saints which deified mortals and created a false reliance on the efficacy of pilgrimage to Sufi shrines. Yaqub did not suggest that he was facing any direct hostility from these reformists but he gestured to their general criticism of Sufism and, since he now believed that he was an integral part of the mystical fraternity, he felt their challenge to his ministry as well.

As a part of a larger mystical fraternity, Yaqub and his son mimed the code of conduct of some of the more famous *dargahs* of Bakhtiyar Kaki and Nizam al-Din Awliya in Delhi. Not the least of these included the introduction of careful gender policing. In 2007, the excesses of a *diwani* pilgrim would not be tolerated within the *dargah* any longer. In fact, the sacred enclosure of the grave was declared out of bounds for women. Instructions on a pillar and the stairs declared that women were prohibited from going up to visit

Photo 22. Instructions on the staircase and the left pillar.

the *pir's* grave and instruction on an adjoining pillar reminded others to cover their heads (see photograph 22). Here Yaqub's son did not depart from his father's vision; he seemed to only extend it. As the reach and influence of Jalal al-Din's shrine expanded and larger amounts of funds diversified the activities within the *dargah*, an effort was made to consolidate its position by integrating aspects of a juridically inspired version of Islam. The newly constructed mosque in the *dargah* also started doubling as a *madrasa* where Muslims families were invited to send their children to learn to read the *Qur'an*. Catechism in the details of the Holy Book did not contradict belief in the Sufi saint whose grace suffused the shrine. Instead, knowledge of the *Qur'an* only protected the believer from innovations and made him into a more accomplished Sufi. While diversifying its role in the lives of the local Muslim community, the presence of the *madrasa* in the shrine also helped in taking the edge off any hostile criticism from reformers like the Deobandis and Barelavis.

Within a couple of decades and without out any claim to antiquity, land and subventions from the Waqf board, the *dargah* of Jalal al-Din Chishti Auliya had gained enough importance to be listed on an internet web site as one of Delhi's important Sufi shrines (http://www.aulia-e-hind.com/dargah/delhi.htm#13). Whereas the shrine of Khwaja Maqbul Shah with all of its potentially viable historical claims disappeared within the renovated Jama Masjid, the *zinda-pir* Jalal al-Din Chishti arose from his repose in the woods of Jahanpanah and through the efforts of his servant, Muhammad Yaqub Chishti, emerged as the dispenser of succour and protection amongst his disciples.

Conclusion

In the spirit of many of the arguments in this book that touched upon the diverse and sometimes unexpected changes that "progress" and "development" wrought on heritage sites and their neighbourhoods in Delhi, the transformations in the Sufi shrines in Delhi can provoke mixed feelings. There is certainly the sense of a huge loss as the character of Khwaja Maqbul Shah's *dargah* altered into the renovated Jama Masjid and the old *baoli* was completely destroyed. A sixteenth century shrine had whimpered to an end, its mystical magic replaced with the stone and mortar of a doctrinal Islam that appeared unbending and intrusive. The sense of loss and its replacement by more universal market forces also seemed to play out in the Jahanpanah forest where, some would argue, an entrepreneur converted an anonymous grave into a flourishing Sufi shrine. The making of the shrine altered the fortunes of its *sajjada nishin*, a seemingly cynical deployment of mysticism and market forces that appeared to be in consonance with the rampant consumerism in the area – exemplified in Delhi's largest shopping mall and the newly resplendent five star hotel in Saket.

And yet beyond this sense of loss – of a time of innocence gone by – there were larger structural features about these developments which should make us pause and reflect about the constitution of

Islam. The shrine of Jalal al-Din Chishti and the Jama Masjid of Khwaja Maqbul Shah in Saket emerged, in their own ways, as extremely venerable and successful centres of Islam where their respective congregations were socialised into related but contrasting versions of Islam. Rather than studying them as discrete entities, they need to be studied within a larger dialectical frame of reference sharing a common spatial and intellectual topography. The triumph of scholastic Islam in the Saket Jama Masjid and of Sufism in the Jahanpanah shrine are reflective of how the multiple strands of Islam continue to flourish and gain adherents within a kilometre of each other. It is the vibrant success of these alterities, each of them deriving their meaning from integral aspects of Islam that mark its resistance to efforts at homogenisation. And as long as these multiplicities continue to flourish in their proximate habitats, Islam and Muslims will remain in [contentious] dialogue with the great traditions that constituted them over time. The cry of "Islam in danger" is articulated only when we are unable to notice and appreciate its divergent practices, assuming for the moment that individuals like the Pradhan Haji Muhammad Jathariya or the servitor of the Jahanpanah shrine, Muhammad Yaqub Chishti, alone speak for the religion. Neither of these venerable masters nor their congregations comprise the "church" of Islam and as we turn to the larger composition of the Muslim community – a huge amorphous entity that is often difficult to imagine – a momentary reflection on the two Sufi shrines in South Delhi helps in bringing into focus the contrasting histories that leant form and substance to Islam and being a Muslim today.

Three Essays Collective focuses on works of scholarship which touch upon issues of contemporary concern. They address a wide range of themes in history, society, politics, culture, education and the media. South Asian themes predominate in, but do not exhaust, the scope of these publications. They are intended to familiarise readers with current debates in their respective fields, even as they enlarge areas of enquiry.

Three Essays
COLLECTIVE

OTHER TITLES

Aijaz Ahmad, *On Communalism and Globalization: Offensives of the Far Right*

Amar Farooqi, *Opium City: The Making of Early Victorian Bombay*

Angana Chatterji, *Violent Gods: Hindu Nationalism in India's Present – Narratives from Orissa*

Archana Prasad, *Against Ecological Romanticism: Verrier Elwin and the Making of an Anti-Modern Tribal Identity*

Ashraf Aziz, *Light of the Universe: Essays on Hindustani Film Music*

Barbara Harriss-White, *India's Market Society: Three Essays in Political Economy*

Biswamoy Pati, *Identity, Hegemony, Resistance: Towards a Social History of Conversions in Orissa, 1800-2000*

Brinda Karat, *Survival and Emancipation: Notes from Indian Women's Struggles*

Colin Leys, *Total Capitalism: Market Politics, Market State*

Eduardo Galeano, *Open Veins of Latin America: Five Centuries of the Pillage of a Continent*

Jackie Assayag and Véronique Bénéï (eds.), *Re-mapping Knowledge: The Making of SouthAsian Studies in India, Europe and America, 19th-20th centuries*

John S Saul, *Development After Globalization: Theory and Practice for an Embattled South in a New Imperial Age*

John S Saul, *Decolonization and Empire: Contesting the Rhetoric and Practice of Resubordination in Southern Africa and Beyond*

KN Panikkar, *An Agenda for Cultural Action and Other Essays*

Kristoffel Lieten, *Views on Development: The Local and the Global in India and Pakistan*

Madhu Trivedi, *The Making of Hindustani Classicism: Music and Performing Arts in North India, 13th–19th Centuries*

Meera Nanda, *Breaking the Spell of Dharma and Other Essays*

Meera Nanda, *The Wrongs of the Religious Right: Reflections on Science, Secularism and Hindutva*

Meeto (Kamaljit Bhasin-Malik), *In the Making: Identity Formation in South Asia*

Mukul Dube, *The Path of the Parivar: Articles on Gujarat and Hindutva*

Omar Khalidi, *Khaki and Ethnic Violence in India: Army, Police and Paramilitary Forces during Communal Riots*

Omar Khalidi, *Muslims in Indian Economy*

Paul R Brass, *Forms of Collective Violence: Riots, Pogroms, and Genocide in Modern India*

Patricia Jeffery and Roger Jeffery, *Confronting Saffron Demography: Religion, Fertility, and Women's Status in India*

Radhika Desai, *Slouching Towards Ayodhya: From Congress to Hindutva in Indian Politics*

Ralph Russell, *Findings, Keepings: The Autobiography of Ralph Russell, Early Years, 1918-1945*

Ralph Russell, *Losses Gains: The Autobiography of Ralph Russell, Middle Years, 1945-1958*

RK Jain, *Indian Transmigrants: Malaysian and Comparative Essays*

Romila Thapar, *The Aryan: Recasting Constructs*

S. Irfan Habib, *To Make the Deaf Hear: Ideology and Programme of Bhagat Singh and His Comrades*

Shereen Ratnagar, *The Other Indians: Essays on Pastoralists and Pre-Historic Tribal People*

Shubh Mathur, *The Everyday Life of Hindu Nationalism: An Ethnographic Account*

Subhash Gatade, *The Saffron Condition*

Sunil Kumar (ed.), *Demolishing Myths or Mosques or Temples: Readings on Hostroy andTemple Desecration in Medieval India*

Utsa Patnaik, *The Republic of Hunger and Other Essays*

Vasudha Dalmia, *Orienting India: European Knowledge Formation in the Eighteenth and Nineteenth Centuries*

Vijay Prashad, *The American Scheme: Three Essays*

Vina Mazumdar, *The Mind and the Medium: Explorations in the Evolution of British Imperial Policy in India*

Zaheer Baber, *Secularism, Communalism and the Intellectuals*